Stick with Carrot

A Practical Guide to Designing Incentives That Actually Work

Jamie L. Bond

ISBN: 979-8-9953924-0-8 (Paperback)

ISBN: 979-8-9953924-1-5 (E-book)

LCCN: 2026907239

Printed in the United States.

First Edition: April 2026

Published by:
path.konkat
PO Box 690961, Charlotte, NC 28227
www.pathkonkat.com

Disclaimer: The information contained in this book is provided for educational and informational purposes only. It is not intended as legal, financial, regulatory, or professional advice.

Examples and scenarios described in this book are intended to illustrate structural patterns in organizational systems. In some cases identifying details have been modified or composite examples have been used.

Contents

Dedication

For Harold — my partner in business and in life.

And for the executive mentors who were always so transparent and generous with their lived experience. This book exists because you shared what you saw.

Acknowledgments

This book was shaped by people who were willing to say what they actually saw.

Harold Manning — you are my first reader, my sharpest critic, and my steadiest partner. Every idea in these pages was tested in conversation with you, often late at night, often more than once. This book would not exist without your patience, your precision, and your willingness to tell me when something wasn't working.

Several executive mentors shaped the thinking behind this book long before it was a manuscript. **Brett Carter**, **Peter Hastings**, **Daniel Woodall** and **Charles Tooman** — each of you, at different moments in my career, chose transparency over ceremony. You generously shared how systems actually operated, not how they were supposed to. That generosity is rare and it made this framework possible.

Finally, to every leader who has ever looked at their own system and said, "This isn't what we designed" — you are the audience this book was written for. The fact that you noticed is where change begins.

How to Read This Book

Most organizations do not fail because people are incompetent or because leaders lack good intentions. In many cases, the individuals involved are acting rationally within the constraints they face. Yet the outcomes the system produces are persistently disappointing: workarounds multiply, innovation stalls, safety deteriorates, performance targets distort behavior, and well-designed programs produce results no one intended.

These patterns are often treated as operational problems. In reality, they are frequently signals of deeper structural misalignment. Workarounds persist not because people resist rules, but because the system's incentives reward outcomes that the formal process cannot reliably produce.

This book examines a simple but powerful idea: many of these failures are produced not by individuals, but by the incentive architecture of the system itself.

Incentives are often discussed as individual mechanisms—a bonus plan, a performance metric, a regulatory rule. When problems appear, organizations tend to adjust these mechanisms: change the metric, tighten the rule, introduce a new control. But these adjustments rarely address the deeper structure that shapes behavior across decisions.

In this book, incentives are defined more precisely as the mechanisms through which system structure creates behavioral pressure. These pressures influence what people prioritize, what risks they are willing to take, and how they interpret success inside the system.

The argument of this book is that these mechanisms operate as part of a broader architecture. That architecture determines the signals the system sends about what actually matters, the risks individuals personally bear when outcomes go wrong, and the pressures that guide decisions across thousands of everyday actions.

When the architecture is coherent, ordinary incentives can produce effective behavior. When it is misaligned, even capable people acting rationally will generate outcomes that appear dysfunctional.

The chapters that follow develop this argument in stages.

The first part of the book examines familiar organizational patterns—workarounds, rational adaptations, and persistent misalignment—and shows how these patterns emerge in real systems. The second part introduces a structural framework for understanding how incentive architecture operates. The third part presents a diagnostic lens for identifying where misalignment resides. The final sections apply this lens across several domains, from corporate performance systems to public policy and algorithmic decision systems.

The goal of the framework is not to prescribe a universal solution. Instead, it provides a way to see how incentives shape behavior within complex systems and how redesign becomes possible once those structures are understood.

PART I

Why Smart Systems Fail Predictably

Show me the incentive and I'll show you the outcome.

Charlie Munger

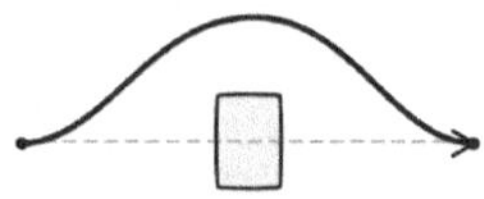

1

The Expensive Workaround

The first sign that something is wrong is rarely a failure. It's usually a workaround.

A nurse keeps a personal notebook because the electronic record is too slow during patient intake. An operations manager maintains a parallel spreadsheet because the official dashboard lags reality by weeks. A customer service team develops informal scripts to navigate a policy that technically exists but functionally blocks resolution. None of these behaviors are documented in the process manual. All of them are essential to getting the work done.

From the outside, these actions often look like resistance. People are "not following the process." They are "going off script." They are "working around the system."

The instinctive managerial response is to tighten controls, reinforce compliance, or retrain staff on the importance of doing things "the right way."

But the behavior itself tells a different story.

People are not irrationally rebelling against well-designed systems. They are responding rationally to the incentives and constraints those systems impose. When formal processes increase effort, delay outcomes, or expose individuals to risk, people adapt. They do so quietly, locally, and efficiently. The workaround is not a failure of discipline. It is evidence of optimization under the conditions that actually exist.

This distinction matters because organizations consistently misdiagnose what they are seeing. They focus on intent — motivation, values, culture — when the more reliable signal is behavior. What people actually do, especially when no one is watching closely, reflects the incentive environment far more clearly than what they say they believe or intend.

Consider what it takes for a workaround to emerge. Someone must decide that following the official process is more costly than deviating from it. That cost may be time, cognitive effort, reputational exposure, or personal risk. The workaround does not appear because someone dislikes the rules. It appears because the rules make the work harder, slower, or more dangerous in ways that matter to the person doing it.

This is not a moral claim. It is a structural one.

People are locally rational within the constraints and incentives they face. They respond to what is rewarded, punished, or ignored in their immediate environment.

When the formal system aligns with the realities of the work, compliance is often effortless.

When it does not, adaptation is inevitable.

Seen this way, workarounds are not anomalies. They are predictable responses to misalignment.

Workarounds are often interpreted as operational shortcuts or resistance to rules. In practice they signal something more structural. When workarounds persist across capable teams and over time, they usually indicate that the formal system is misaligned with the outcomes it claims to pursue. Actors are not rejecting the objective; they are adapting to the pressures the system actually creates.

A workaround survives because it helps people deliver results the formal process cannot reliably produce. The system may prescribe one path, but incentives—implicit or explicit—reward success through another. In this sense, recurring workarounds are not merely operational anomalies. They are diagnostic signals that the underlying incentive structure is pushing behavior away from the formal design.

In many organizations, leaders believe they are managing through formal structures: policies, workflows, performance metrics, and systems of record. But what actually governs day-to-day behavior is something else entirely. It is the combination of time pressure, accountability structures, measurement regimes, and informal consequences that shape what feels safe, efficient, or necessary in the moment.

This is why observed behavior is more diagnostic than stated intent. People may sincerely endorse organizational values, customer priorities, or safety goals. They may repeat them accurately in meetings and surveys. Yet when the system makes adherence costly and deviation cheap — or at least invisible — behavior will diverge from rhetoric. Not because people are dishonest, but because incentives are.

The gap between what organizations say they value and what they systematically reward is where workarounds live.

Take a common administrative workflow. A form is required before an action can be taken. The form exists for good reasons: traceability, auditability, consistency. But the form takes time, requires information that is often unavailable at the point of use, and creates a visible record that can later be scrutinized if something goes wrong. Completing it delays resolution. Skipping it, or completing it retroactively, gets the job done.

Over time, people learn what the system actually responds to. They learn which delays matter and which violations are overlooked. They learn where enforcement is strict and where it is nominal. They learn what creates risk for them personally and what does not. The workaround is not invented in defiance of the system. It is discovered through experience with it.

Once discovered, it spreads.

These adaptations are often informal, undocumented, and invisible to leadership. They exist in side conversations, personal tools, and tacit knowledge passed from one employee to another. They allow the organization to function despite its formal design. They also create a growing gap between how work is imagined and how it is done.

This gap is expensive.

The costs are rarely captured in budgets or dashboards. They show up as duplicated effort, shadow systems, brittle processes, and latent risk. When people maintain parallel tools, data fragments. When steps are skipped or reordered, accountability becomes ambiguous. When work depends on individual ingenuity rather than system reliability, performance becomes fragile.

Yet these costs remain hidden precisely because the workaround is effective. It masks the underlying misalignment. Things appear to be working, so the incentive to investigate diminishes. Leaders see outcomes, not the informal labor required to produce them.

This is where misinterpretation becomes systematic.

From a leadership perspective, workarounds often look like exceptions. They are framed as edge cases, training gaps, or compliance issues. The assumption is that the core system is sound, and the deviation is the problem. Correct the behavior, and performance will improve.

But this framing reverses cause and effect.

The behavior exists because the system imposes costs that make deviation rational. Eliminating the workaround without addressing the misalignment that produced it does not restore order. It shifts the cost back onto the individual. In some cases, it simply drives the workaround further underground.

This is why efforts to "crack down" on informal practices often fail. They target the visible symptom while leaving the incentive structure intact. People still face the same pressures. They still need to get the work done. They just become more careful about how and when they adapt.

Over time, organizations develop a curious duality. The formal system exists on paper and in presentations. The informal system does the real work. Leaders interact primarily with the former and infer intent, commitment, and performance from it. The latter remains largely invisible until something breaks.

When failures occur, they are often attributed to human error or cultural weakness. Why didn't people follow the process? Why didn't they raise concerns? Why didn't they escalate earlier?

These questions assume that the system was neutral and that deviation was optional. They overlook the fact that the system itself shaped what was rational to do at each step.

Workarounds, then, are not signs of dysfunction in isolation. They are signals. They indicate where formal design and operational reality are misaligned. They show where incentives, constraints, and information flows are producing predictable adaptation.

This is why misalignment is more costly than it appears. It does not simply reduce efficiency. It forces the organization to rely on invisible labor, informal coordination, and personal risk-taking to function. It erodes the reliability of data, the integrity of controls, and the credibility of governance structures.

Most importantly, it distorts diagnosis.

When leaders look at outcomes without understanding the adaptations beneath them, they draw the wrong conclusions. They attribute success to policy and failure to people. They reinforce structures that are being quietly bypassed and penalize behaviors that are keeping the system afloat.

The tragedy is not that workarounds exist. It is that they are misunderstood.

Once you see workarounds as rational responses to incentive misalignment, a different diagnostic lens becomes available. Instead of asking why people won't comply, you ask what compliance costs them. Instead of asking why the process isn't followed, you ask what following it makes harder. Instead of interpreting behavior as resistance, you treat it as evidence.

This shift does not require cynicism about values or intent. It requires realism about structure.

People generally want to do competent work. They want to avoid unnecessary risk. They want to be effective within the constraints they face. When systems make those goals incompatible with formal procedures, adaptation is not a failure of character. It is a feature of human systems.

And it recurs.

The same pattern appears across industries, functions, and technologies. Whenever formal design diverges from operational reality, people bridge the gap. They always have. The specifics change. The logic does not.

This is the expensive workaround. Not because it is irrational or malicious, but because it is necessary. It is the price organizations pay for misalignment — and the bill is almost always higher than it looks.

Flagship Case

The organization did everything right — or so it thought.

After years of deferred modernization, leadership approved a major digital transformation for its field operations. The new system promised real-time data, automated workflows, predictive maintenance, and fewer errors. It was expensive, ambitious, and branded internally as "transformational." Consultants were hired. Training sessions were run. Dashboards showed progress. From the outside, it looked like momentum.

Six months after deployment, the system was technically live. And functionally irrelevant.

Field technicians had learned how to bypass most of the automation and operate the system in manual mode. Critical decisions were made the old way. Data was entered late or not at all. The new platform became, in practice, a far more expensive version of the legacy system — without the promised benefits.

Leadership's diagnosis was swift and familiar: resistance to change.

The remedy followed predictably. More training. Stronger mandates. Clearer expectations. Subtle threats about performance reviews. None of it worked.

The problem was not resistance. It was incentives.

The Stated Goal vs. the Rational Choice

The stated goal of the transformation was straightforward: improve efficiency, reduce errors, and modernize operations through automation. But the system's incentive architecture rewarded something else entirely: speed, risk avoidance, and short-term performance under pressure.

From the technician's perspective, the rational choice was obvious. Manual operation was faster. It reduced the risk of visible errors. It avoided being the first to fail publicly with a new tool. And it aligned with what supervisors actually cared about when outages occurred: restoring service quickly, not experimenting with software.

No amount of exhortation could override that calculus.

What the Incentive Architecture Revealed

When the initiative is mapped against the Incentive Architecture™, the outcome stops looking mysterious.

Structural incentives placed decision rights for system design and rollout far from the field. Executives and program leaders bore little operational risk if adoption failed, while technicians bore immediate consequences if automation slowed response times. Authority and accountability were misaligned from the start.

Economic incentives reinforced this imbalance. Compensation and performance metrics rewarded throughput and uptime, not system adoption or learning. Capital deployment itself was treated as success, regardless of whether benefits materialized. Using the new system carried no upside and meaningful downside.

Temporal incentives were perhaps the most damaging. Deployment milestones and quarterly reporting cycles rewarded rapid rollout, not gradual adoption. The organization expected long-term efficiency gains while punishing short-term disruption — the exact opposite of what learning-intensive change requires.

Behavioral incentives sealed the outcome. The automated workflows added friction. Manual overrides were always available. Data entry increased cognitive load in high-pressure situations. Workarounds were not only possible; they were inevitable.

Finally, **social and reputational incentives** reinforced the pattern. Experienced technicians earned status by "getting the job done" under difficult conditions, not by experimenting with new tools. Early failures with the system were visible and quietly stigmatized. Adoption was reported upward, but actual usage was neither visible nor rewarded.

Across every layer, the system made the same thing rational: bypass the automation and move on.

Why Enforcement Failed — and Always Will

From management's perspective, the response made sense. If people are not using the system, require them to use it. But enforcement operates at the top of the incentive stack. It is a stick applied to social and behavioral layers.

The problem was that lower layers — structure, economics, and time horizons — were actively pushing in the opposite direction. The result was predictable: superficial compliance, creative workarounds, and increasingly elaborate reporting that masked reality.

The more leadership pushed, the more technicians optimized around the system.

This is the defining pattern of incentive failure: when enforcement rises, gaming follows.

The Real Cost of Getting Incentives Wrong

The most expensive part of this failure was not the technology itself. It was the opportunity cost.

The organization paid for a system capable of delivering meaningful operational insight but structured incentives so that insight was never generated. It incurred the political and cultural cost of a "failed transformation" without ever addressing the actual cause. And it reinforced a dangerous lesson for the workforce: that the safest response to future initiatives is quiet circumvention.

From the outside, the story looks like a technology failure. From inside the incentive architecture, it looks like success. The system produced exactly what it rewarded.

The Diagnostic Shift That Changes Everything

Once the problem is reframed as incentive architecture — not culture or competence — the path forward changes.

The critical question is no longer "How do we get people to use the system?" It becomes: What would have to be true, at each layer of the incentive architecture, for using the system to be the rational choice?

That question points to different interventions entirely: shifting decision rights, absorbing early risk at higher levels, protecting learning periods from performance penalties, redesigning defaults, and redefining what earns status in the field.

Those are harder changes. They are also the only ones that work.

Why This Case Matters

This pattern repeats across sectors. In corporate transformations. In public programs. In regulatory reform. In technology adoption. Whenever leaders mistake the wrapper for the mechanism, outcomes disappoint and blame follows.

The lesson is not that automation is hard or that people resist change. It is that systems do what their incentive architectures tell them to do.

Sticks create short-term obedience. *Carrots* create long-term alignment.

And without alignment, transformation is just an expensive illusion.

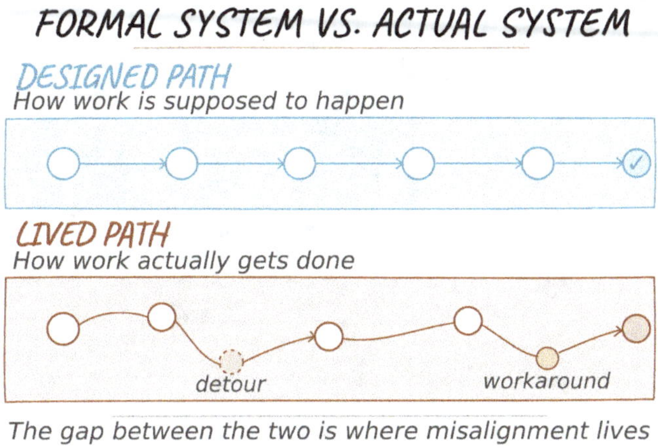

***Figure 1.1:** Formal systems describe how work is supposed to happen. Actual systems reveal how work does happen once incentives, risk, and consequence enter the picture.*

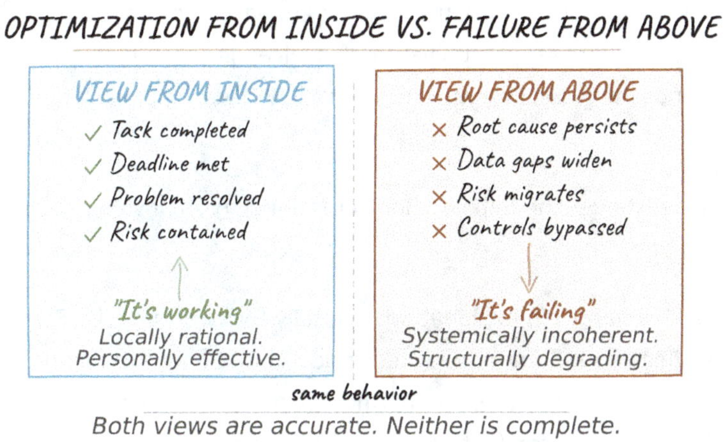

***Figure 1.2:** The same behavior can look like success from inside the system and failure from above. Perspective determines interpretation.*

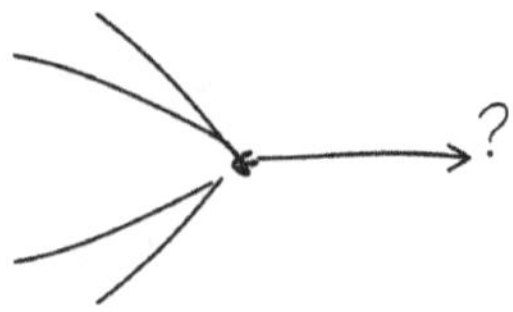

2

The Rationality Trap

There is a familiar frustration that appears in organizations when outcomes disappoint. Everyone involved is capable. Everyone understands the goals. Everyone appears aligned. And yet the same results recur.

From a distance, the behavior looks irrational. From inside the system, it feels unavoidable.

When this happens, explanations typically focus on people. Someone misunderstood. Someone lacked motivation. Someone failed to prioritize correctly. Culture, commitment, or intent is questioned. These explanations are comforting because they preserve a belief that the system itself is sound.

They rarely hold up.

When the same patterns persist across teams, roles, and leadership changes, it becomes difficult to attribute failure to ignorance or apathy. Highly capable people repeat the same choices even after they have been explained, trained, and corrected. At that point, the problem is no longer individual judgment.

The error is in how rationality is being assessed.

Behavior inside organizations is rarely arbitrary. Even when actions appear inconsistent or counterproductive from the outside, they usually reflect rational adaptation to the pressures individuals face. Three pressures are especially influential: what the system measures, what it rewards or punishes, and what risks individuals personally bear.

Together these pressures shape the practical boundaries of decision-making. People learn quickly which outcomes are visible, which consequences are tied to performance, and which mistakes carry personal cost. Once these signals become clear, behavior tends to adjust accordingly. Understanding these pressures is therefore essential to understanding why systems produce the behaviors they do.

People are locally rational within the constraints and incentives they face. They make decisions that make sense given the information available, the pressures they experience, and the consequences they anticipate. What looks irrational at the system level is often prudent at the individual level.

A manager delays escalation not because the issue is unimportant, but because escalation carries personal risk and uncertain payoff. A team favors incremental delivery over a bolder initiative not because it lacks ambition, but because failure is remembered more clearly than success is rewarded.

These choices are not anomalies. They are predictable responses to local conditions.

This is where diagnosis often fails.

Observed outcomes are attributed to values or intent because those are visible and discussable. Surveys are run. Messages are reinforced. When behavior does not change, frustration grows.

But stated intent is a weak predictor of action when incentives conflict.

Observed behavior is evidence of incentives, not intent. People can sincerely endorse goals and still act against them when alignment carries personal cost. Under pressure, individuals economize. They avoid unnecessary risk. They attend to what is visible, enforceable, and immediate. These are not flaws. They are adaptations.

Capability does not eliminate this dynamic. It often sharpens it. Skilled actors become better at navigating constraints and optimizing within them. They do what works, even when they recognize that local success may undermine global outcomes.

The result is an inversion that feels perplexing from above. Leadership communicates priorities clearly. Teams acknowledge them. Behavior remains unchanged. Each side interprets the other as missing something obvious.

What is missing is not clarity. It is alignment.

Persistent outcomes reveal the incentive environment more reliably than any articulation of intent. Individual decisions can almost always be justified in isolation. The irrationality appears only in aggregation.

At the system level, locally rational choices can produce results no one wants. Innovation stalls. Risk accumulates quietly. Metrics improve while reality degrades. Accountability exists formally and dissolves operationally.

Attempts to correct this usually intensify pressure on individuals. Values are restated. Training is added. Expectations are sharpened. Sometimes enforcement increases. These efforts shift cost onto individuals without changing the conditions shaping behavior.

People cannot consistently act against their local incentives without paying a price. Some absorb that cost temporarily. Most adapt. The system adjusts accordingly.

This is the rationality trap: mistaking sincere intent for sufficient cause, and mistaking predictable adaptation for failure.

Once this is seen, interpretation changes. Instead of asking why people will not do what makes sense, the question becomes what sense the system is asking them to make. Behavior stops looking like resistance and starts reading as evidence.

The inevitability is not failure. It is response.

As long as incentives and constraints remain as they are, intelligent, well-intentioned people will continue to produce outcomes they do not endorse. Not because they are irrational, but because they are not free.

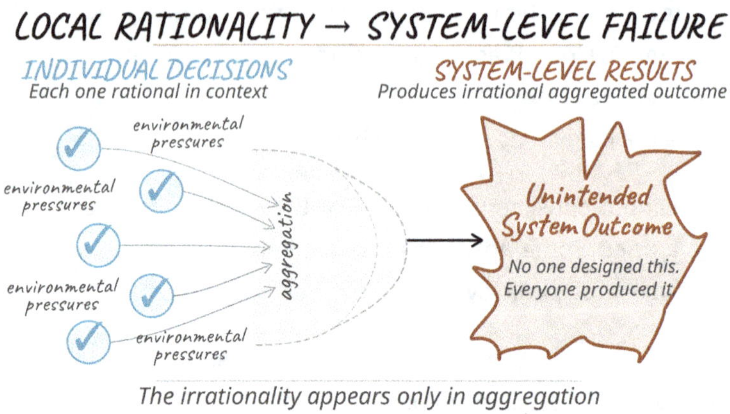

Figure 2.1: *Individually rational decisions can aggregate into outcomes no one intends.*

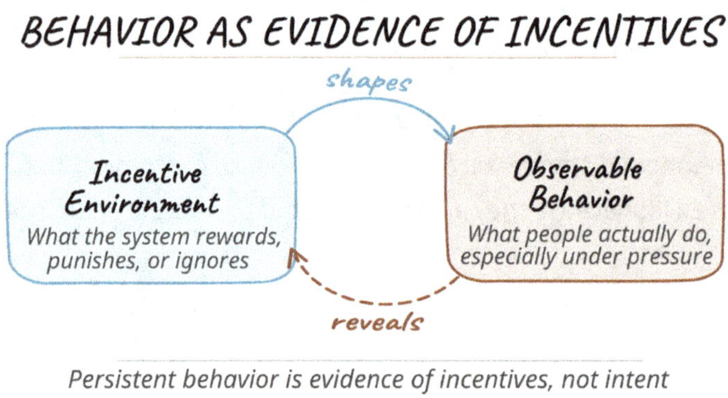

Figure 2.2: *Persistent behavior is a more reliable indicator of incentives than stated priorities or expressed intent.*

The Escalation That Never Happened

In a large organization, an issue surfaces repeatedly at the front line. Each instance is small enough to manage locally. Escalation would require additional documentation, exposure to scrutiny, and the possibility of being seen as unable to resolve problems independently.

Managers understand that escalation is encouraged in principle, but they also know that it creates reputational risk with uncertain payoff. Over time, the issue is managed quietly. Workarounds develop. Local fixes are applied.

From above, leadership sees no signal that intervention is needed. From below, escalation feels unnecessary and risky. When the issue eventually surfaces at scale, the question asked is why no one spoke up sooner. From inside the system, many did—just not in ways that crossed the thresholds required to trigger action. Each choice was reasonable. The outcome was not.

Reference: Local Rationality (Ch 2)

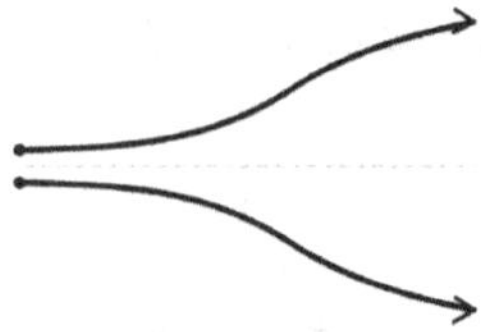

3

When Alignment Breaks

When outcomes disappoint, organizations often return to explanations rooted in character. If results fall short, people must lack skill, commitment, or alignment with values. Culture becomes the explanation of last resort.

This framing persists because it preserves faith in intent.

It also fails repeatedly.

Across sectors and systems, the same patterns appear. Rules are followed in ways that undermine stated goals. Performance improves on paper while risk accumulates elsewhere. No one claims responsibility for outcomes everyone can see coming. Each instance is explainable on its own. Together, they indicate something structural.

The issue is not whether incentives exist. It is whether they agree.

In this book, alignment refers specifically to structural incentives directing behavior toward intended outcomes. It does not refer to shared intentions, cultural cohesion, or agreement about goals. Organizations may have strong values, capable leaders, and sincere commitment to outcomes, yet still experience misalignment if the structure of incentives consistently pushes decisions in another direction.

Misalignment arises in complex systems where multiple actors make interdependent decisions under imperfect visibility. Each incentive is introduced for a reason. Each metric solves a past problem. Over time, these incentives begin to pull behavior in different directions.

Shared intent does not resolve this.

Sales organizations offer a familiar illustration. Leadership emphasizes long-term customer trust and suitability. Sales teams are evaluated and rewarded on volume closed. Over time, behavior shifts toward deals that maximize near-term numbers, even as rhetoric about customer outcomes intensifies. No one disputes the stated goal. The system simply makes a different behavior safer to demonstrate.

People can agree on goals and still act at cross purposes when incentives conflict. Alignment is not about belief. It is about whether the system makes coordinated action possible.

Misalignment rarely announces itself as disagreement. It appears as a series of reasonable local optimizations that aggregate into unreasonable outcomes. Speed is rewarded in one place, accuracy in another, compliance in a third. Each signal makes sense. Together, they do not.

Measurement accelerates this dynamic. Metrics are not neutral observers. Once tied to evaluation or reward, they become behavioral magnets. When a measure becomes a target, effort shifts toward protecting the proxy. The goal remains rhetorically intact while decisions increasingly reflect what is safest to demonstrate.

This is often labeled gaming. The term implies bad faith. In practice, it is adaptation. People respond rationally to what the system rewards.

When incentives disagree, behavior resolves the conflict.

The strongest signals dominate. Incentives closest to consequence — those that affect time, exposure, reputation, or compensation — exert the greatest pull. Distant intentions matter, but they matter less when they compete with immediate pressure.

"This is why misalignment produces optimization rather than confusion. People are rarely unsure what to do. They are clear about which actions carry risk and which do not. They choose accordingly.

From above, the logic is obscured. Leaders see outcomes that contradict stated goals and assume misunderstanding or resistance. Inside the system, the logic is explicit. The safest incentive wins.

Misalignment persists because it is not owned by any single decision. It emerges from accumulation. New incentives are added without removing old ones. Controls multiply. Accountability overlaps. People learn to navigate the resulting field by prioritizing what is most enforceable and least risky.

Efforts to fix failure by strengthening incentives often worsen the problem. Adding targets or controls introduces new forces into an already conflicted system. Something improves. Something else degrades. The disagreement remains.

The appeal of culture-based explanations lies in their simplicity. If behavior reflects values, changing values should change outcomes. Misalignment breaks that assumption. It shows how behavior can diverge from intent even when intent is sincere and shared.

Most systems do not fail because incentives are weak. They fail because incentives disagree. When they do, the system adapts. Workarounds emerge. Metrics drift. Risk migrates. From inside, this feels like competence. From outside, it looks like dysfunction.

Both are true.

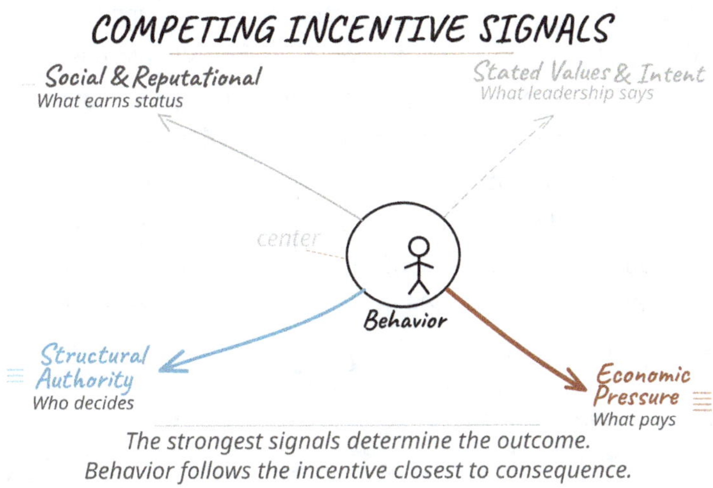

Figure 3.1: *When incentives pull in different directions, behavior resolves the conflict by following the strongest signals.*

When Everyone Agrees and Nothing Changes

In post-mortems, teams often report broad agreement on goals. Quality matters. Safety matters. Long-term value matters. Yet behavior continues to track short-term metrics, compliance thresholds, or throughput targets. This disconnect is frequently attributed to weak culture or inconsistent messaging. What is missed is that agreement does not resolve incentive conflict. When incentives disagree, behavior does not average them. It selects among them. People learn quickly which signals carry consequence and which do not. Alignment fails not because people are confused, but because they are clear about which priorities are enforceable. Shared intent exists alongside structurally opposed incentives, and the latter quietly win.

Reference: Misalignment (Ch 3)

PART II

Seeing the System Beneath the System

The fish is the last to know it is swimming in water.

Marshall McLuhan

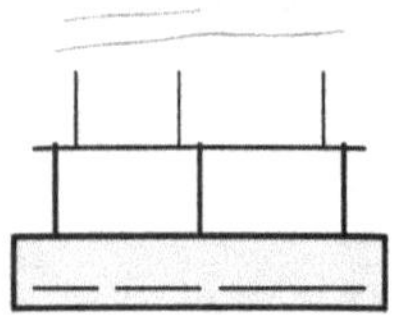

4

Incentives Are Architecture, Not Programs

When organizations want to change behavior, they usually reach for programs.

Training initiatives are launched. Values are refreshed. Communications intensify. Incentives are adjusted in narrow, visible ways. These actions are legible and reassuring. They look like progress.

They also fail with consistency.

When behavior does not change, failure is attributed to execution. The program was not strong enough. The message did not land. The culture work needs reinforcement.

The premise remains untouched: if the intervention were better, behavior would follow.

What goes unexamined is the assumption beneath it.

Programs operate at the surface. They assume behavior is discretionary — responsive to instruction or motivation. They treat incentives as levers rather than as conditions that shape which choices are viable in the first place.

Structure operates earlier.

People may agree with a program's goal. They may want it to succeed. But when compliance carries friction or exposure, intent yields to reality. The system defines the cost of alignment before any message is delivered.

This distinction matters.

Incentives are not add-ons layered onto neutral systems. They are embedded conditions that shape effort, risk, and consequence. They determine what feels safe, rewarded, or punishable. They define what "good performance" means in practice, not in principle.

This is why programmatic fixes disappoint. They compete with forces they do not control.

Culture initiatives lose when incentives contradict them. Training fails when people already understand the right action but know it will cost them. Incentive programs misfire when they target one behavior without accounting for the pressures surrounding it.

The result is a familiar pattern. One outcome improves while another worsens. Compliance rises as responsiveness falls. Metrics strengthen as candor erodes. Each effect is explicable.

Together, they indicate architectural conflict.

Incentives operate through multiple interacting conditions. Some are explicit. Others are learned through experience. Some are immediate. Others are distant. What matters is their relative strength.

Certain incentives are closer to consequence. They are enforced more consistently. They carry sharper penalties. These dominate regardless of how clearly higher-level intentions are articulated.

People orient toward what has proven reliable. They learn which signals can be ignored and which cannot. Over time, behavior aligns with the architecture, not the program.

This explains why intensified effort can worsen outcomes. Additional reporting increases risk. New targets narrow attention. Oversight layers add weight without support. The system becomes harder to inhabit without becoming more coherent.

Programs persist because architecture is harder to see and change. Programs can be launched. Architecture accumulates. Each component once made sense.

Together, they quietly dictate behavior.

The pattern emerging across the first three chapters follows a consistent logic. Workarounds appear when formal processes fail to produce the outcomes organizations require. Competent actors respond by adapting their behavior in ways that allow them to succeed within the pressures they face.

Over time these adaptations reveal deeper structural issues. Alignment breaks not because people misunderstand objectives, but because the system directs behavior toward other priorities. The resulting behaviors are rational responses to the system as it actually operates.

If behavior is consistently shaped by these pressures, then incentives cannot be understood only as isolated programs or policies. They must be understood as part of the structure of the system itself. In other words, incentives operate as architecture.

Once incentives are understood as architecture, failure looks different. Behavior diverges from intent not because people are unwilling, but because the system makes some choices easier and safer than others.

This reframing is uncomfortable because it removes a convenient fiction: that behavior can be fixed independently of structure. Systems behave as they are built to behave. Once that becomes visible, it is difficult to unsee.

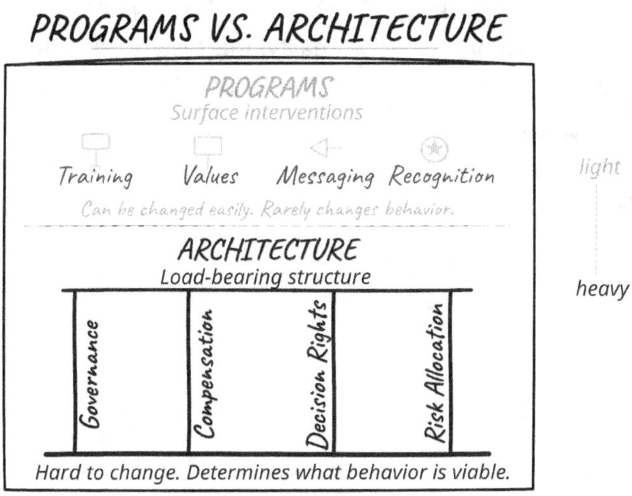

Figure 4.1: *Programs act on the surface of systems. Architecture shapes which choices are viable before programs begin.*

Training Didn't Fail

An organization invests heavily in training. Employees can articulate correct procedures and desired behaviors. Assessments show high comprehension. Yet observed behavior remains unchanged. Additional training is prescribed. Messaging is reinforced. The assumption is that behavior will follow understanding. What goes unexamined is whether the system makes the trained behavior viable. If following procedure increases time, exposure, or error visibility without reducing risk elsewhere, training competes with structure. When behavior does not change, the failure is attributed to resistance or fatigue. In reality, the system has taught people something different through experience. Training did not fail. It was overruled.

Reference: Architecture vs. Programs (Ch 4)

5

The Incentive Architecture™

By this point, a pattern should feel familiar.

Efforts to change behavior keep failing, not because people are stubborn or misguided, but because the system quietly makes certain choices safer, easier, or more rational than others. Training helps briefly. Culture initiatives inspire temporarily. New programs launch with energy and fade with frustration. Outcomes drift back to form.

What's been missing is not commitment or intelligence. It's a way of seeing how incentives actually operate.

Incentives themselves are not a new concept. Economists, management scholars, and organizational theorists have long examined how rewards, penalties, and accountability structures influence behavior.

Most of this work, however, focuses on incentives as discrete mechanisms—programs, compensation structures, or policy tools designed to influence particular actions.

This book approaches incentives from a different angle. Instead of asking how individual incentives influence behavior, it asks how systems create patterns of behavioral pressure across many decisions simultaneously. The focus is therefore not incentives as programs, but incentives as architecture.

Viewed through this lens, incentives become structural features of a system that continuously shape how actors interpret priorities, risk, and success. The Incentive Architecture framework that follows provides a way to see—and design—those structures more clearly.

The Incentive Architecture™ is not a theory of human behavior. It is a lens for understanding system behavior. It does not explain why people think what they think. It explains why systems reliably produce outcomes that no one explicitly designed, endorsed, or intended.

In everyday language the term incentive is often used broadly to describe anything that influences behavior. In this book the term is used more precisely. Incentives do not refer to everything within a system. They refer specifically to the mechanisms that translate system structure into behavioral pressure.

These mechanisms determine which actions become easier, safer, faster, or more rewarding for individuals inside the system. When these pressures consistently guide behavior toward intended outcomes, incentives are aligned. When they push behavior in other directions, misalignment emerges.

Incentives do not act as isolated tools. They function as an embedded structure — an architecture — that shapes what behavior is rewarded, punished, or made risky.

That structure operates through five distinct but interacting layers. Once seen together, they explain why alignment is fragile, why misalignment is common, and why fixes applied at the surface rarely hold.

The Incentive Architecture framework introduced in this chapter organizes the structural forces that shape behavior within systems. Each layer represents a distinct mechanism through which behavioral pressure is created and sustained.

These layers should not be interpreted as abstract categories. They represent practical control points in system design—places where decisions about measurement, authority, accountability, and consequence translate directly into behavioral incentives. Understanding these mechanisms makes it possible to see how systems guide behavior across thousands of everyday decisions.

The first layer is **Structural Incentives.**

Structural incentives control who has authority, who bears responsibility, and who is exposed when things go wrong. They are embedded in organizational charts, decision rights, approval pathways, and governance arrangements. This layer determines who can say yes, who must say no, and who absorbs the consequences of either. It is powerful because it defines accountability before any individual decision is made. When failure occurs, this layer decides where blame lands and where it does not. Structural failure often looks like stalled decisions, excessive escalation, or chronic avoidance of ownership. When responsibility is diffuse and consequences are concentrated, people learn quickly what not to touch. Behavior follows structure.

The second layer is **Economic Incentives.**

Economic incentives control how money, resources, and formal rewards are allocated. Compensation, bonuses, budgets, and financial targets live here. This layer is powerful because it is explicit and legible.

People know when economic incentives apply, and they know when they do not. Failure at this layer often looks like optimizing for measured financial outcomes at the expense of broader objectives, or protecting budget lines even when doing so harms system performance. When economic rewards conflict with stated goals, economic reality wins. Behavior aligns with what pays.

The third layer is **Temporal Incentives.**

Temporal incentives control how time is experienced and valued. They shape planning horizons, evaluation cycles, deadlines, and pacing. This layer determines whether near-term performance is rewarded more than long-term resilience, and whether patience is feasible or penalized. It is powerful because time pressure compresses choice. Under tight timelines, options narrow and risk tolerance drops. Failure here often looks like chronic short-termism: quick wins crowd out durable solutions, and urgent work displaces important work. When consequences arrive later than evaluations, behavior shifts toward immediacy.

The fourth layer is **Behavioral Incentives**.

Behavioral incentives control friction, effort, and cognitive load. They are embedded in tools, processes, interfaces, and workflows. This layer shapes what is easy, what is exhausting, and what is error-prone. It is powerful because people conserve attention and energy. When the right behavior requires more effort than the wrong one, adaptation follows.

Failure at this layer often looks like workarounds, shortcuts, and informal systems that bypass official processes. When doing the "right" thing is harder than doing something else, people choose the path of least resistance.

The fifth layer is **Social & Reputational Incentives**.

Social and reputational incentives control status, belonging, credibility, and exposure to judgment. They determine whose voice carries weight, whose mistakes are forgiven, and whose actions are remembered. This layer is powerful because social consequences are immediate and personal. Failure often looks like silence, conformity, or risk avoidance in the presence of uncertainty. When speaking up threatens reputation or standing, discretion replaces candor. Behavior aligns with what preserves social safety.

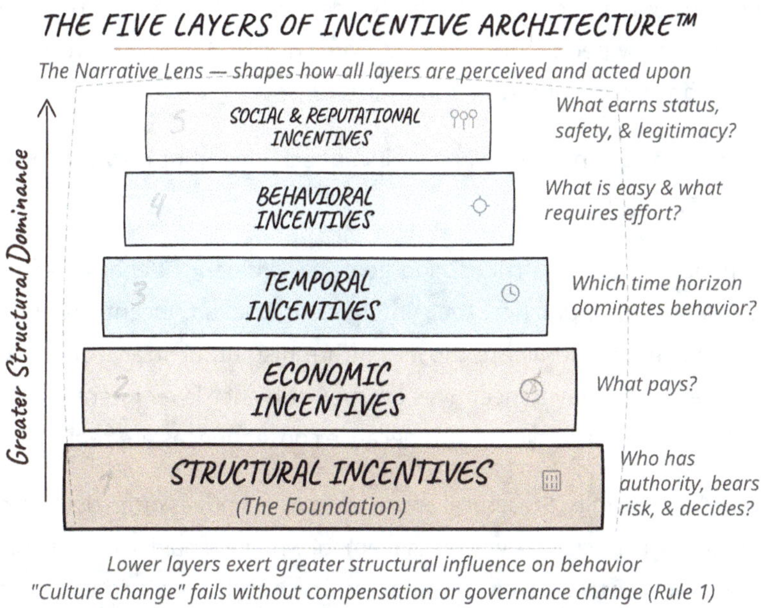

Figure 5.1: *Incentive architecture operates across multiple layers that jointly shape behavior, often without explicit coordination.*

Each of these layers shapes behavior by controlling what is rewarded, punished, or made risky. None of them operate in isolation. Together, they form the incentive architecture of a system.

In many organizations, incentives are addressed primarily through programs—bonus structures, performance initiatives, or targeted behavioral campaigns. These programs attempt to modify behavior in specific situations or around particular objectives.

Architecture operates at a different level. Rather than modifying isolated behaviors, it shapes the system of pressures that actors face across decisions. When incentives are embedded in system architecture, they influence how people prioritize, interpret risk, and allocate effort long before any formal program is introduced.

What matters is not just what exists at each layer, but how the layers interact.

In theory, intentions, values, and goals can influence behavior across all five layers. In practice, their influence is uneven. Incentives closer to consequence dominate those that are distant, abstract, or weakly enforced. Lower-layer incentives overpower higher-layer intentions not because people are cynical, but because consequences are real.

Consider proximity. Structural and economic incentives often determine immediate exposure — who gets blamed, who gets paid, who gets promoted. Temporal incentives compress or extend the window in which decisions are judged.

Behavioral incentives shape the effort required to comply. Social incentives impose instant feedback through approval or disapproval. Higher-layer intentions, such as mission statements or strategic priorities, operate at a remove. They matter, but they do not bite in the same way.

This dominance is not moral and not optional. It is mechanical.

When incentives disagree across layers, people do not average them. They prioritize. They follow the strongest, safest, or most immediate signal. A stated value loses to a compensation metric. A long-term goal loses to a quarterly review. A safety principle loses to a workflow that punishes delay. Each choice is rational in context. Aggregated, they produce outcomes that appear incoherent.

This is why misalignment across layers explains so much apparent failure.

A program can be well-designed at one layer and undermined by another. A culture initiative may encourage speaking up, while structural incentives punish escalation. A performance dashboard may highlight quality, while economic incentives reward throughput. A strategy may emphasize innovation, while temporal incentives penalize experimentation. None of these systems are broken individually. Together, they disagree.

When disagreement exists, behavior resolves it.

This resolution often looks like gaming, optimization, or quiet avoidance. These are not signs of confusion. They are signs that the architecture is working exactly as built. People are responding to the strongest incentives available to them.

Understanding this changes the diagnostic task.

Instead of asking whether incentives are strong enough, the question becomes whether they are aligned. Instead of asking why people ignore values, the question becomes which layers contradict them. Instead of attributing failure to culture or competence, the focus shifts to structure.

The Incentive Architecture™ makes failures predictable because it makes incentives legible. Once the layers are visible, patterns that once seemed idiosyncratic begin to repeat. Workarounds recur. Metrics drift.

Risk accumulates. Silence spreads. Each symptom maps back to a layer where incentives conflict.

This does not mean every failure can be explained by a single layer. Most cannot. The architecture matters precisely because it is layered. Misalignment often spans multiple layers at once, reinforcing itself.

A process that is cognitively burdensome, evaluated on speed, overseen by distant decision-makers, and socially risky to challenge will reliably produce adaptation. No amount of training will prevent it. No amount of messaging will override it. The system has already decided what behavior makes sense.

Diagnosis must therefore precede redesign.

Until the incentive architecture is understood, changes are guesswork. Programs are added without knowing what they must compete against. Metrics are introduced without understanding what they will displace. Accountability is tightened without seeing where risk will migrate.

The architecture does not need to be admired or defended. It needs to be seen.

Once seen, it becomes clear why so many well-intentioned efforts fail in familiar ways. The system is not resisting change. It is enforcing coherence among its incentives.

That coherence may not match the organization's stated goals. But it will prevail until alignment replaces disagreement.

Seeing the Incentive Architecture™ does not solve problems on its own. It does something more basic and more necessary. It gives you a way to understand why the system behaves as it does — and why it will continue to do so until its underlying structure changes.

6

Two Rules That Explain Most Failures

The two rules described in this chapter should be understood as recurring structural patterns rather than universal laws. They are derived from observing how systems behave across many organizations, industries, and policy environments.

These rules function as diagnostic simplifications. They help explain why certain incentive failures appear repeatedly even in well-intentioned systems. By identifying these patterns, readers can more quickly recognize the structural dynamics that drive many persistent organizational problems.

Complexity is real. The layers are real. The interactions are real. But what they reduce to is simpler than most people expect. Under pressure, you do not need a full model in your head.

You need two rules you can hold onto when the explanations get emotional and the fixes get performative.

Rule 1: Lower layers dominate higher layers.

"Lower" does not mean less important. It means closer to consequence. It means nearer to what people experience immediately: workload, approvals, money, risk, exposure, status. "Higher" means farther away: stated values, long-term strategy, official priorities, aspirational culture.

This is not cynical. It is structural.

When incentives are closest to consequence, they behave like gravity. They pull behavior toward what is safe and rewarded in the near field, even when the distant story says something else. People can sincerely endorse the distant story. They can repeat it accurately. They can believe it. But they still have to live in the near field.

A team can be told to "prioritize quality," and still learn that missed deadlines trigger escalation while defects are quietly absorbed. The local consequence is clear. The behavior follows it.

This is why intent, culture, and values lose when they are overridden. Not because they are meaningless, but because they are outcompeted. A principle that costs nothing is easy to hold. A principle that costs time, money, or personal exposure is an incentive. If a higher-layer intention asks for sacrifice and a lower-layer incentive punishes it, the intention becomes a slogan. The system has already decided which signal is real.

Rule 2: Misalignment produces gaming, not confusion.

When outcomes are ugly, "confusion" is a comforting explanation. It implies that if we explain more clearly, train more thoroughly, or communicate more often, people will comply. It treats behavior as a misunderstanding.

But most gaming is not misunderstanding. It is adaptation.

Gaming is what happens when people confront conflicting incentives and choose the option that is safest, most rewarded, or least punishable. It is not deviance. It is problem-solving within constraints. The system gets the behavior it rewards, even when that behavior looks strange from above.

A metric is introduced to improve performance. It becomes tied to review conversations. People learn that the metric matters more than the underlying intent. They adjust what they report, what they prioritize, what they spend time on. They are not confused about what leadership wants. They are clear about what the system rewards.

This is why gaming behavior is diagnostic evidence of system design. It is feedback. It tells you which incentives are actually binding. It shows you where the system has created a rational path that bypasses the goal while still satisfying the proxy.

These two rules reinforce each other.

Misalignment creates competing incentives. Rule 1 tells you how the competition resolves. The lower-layer incentives win. Rule 2 tells you what winning looks like. It looks like optimization around the conflict. People route around the intention and toward the enforceable signal.

This is also why fixing one layer often worsens outcomes elsewhere.

When a system is misaligned, changing one incentive rarely removes the conflict. It shifts it. Tighten one target and attention moves away from what is now unrewarded. Add a new control and people invest in compliance behavior that reduces exposure, not necessarily risk. Intensify a value message and it collides with the same near-field incentives as before.

When leaders describe fixes "backfiring," they often mean something simpler: the rules were ignored. The system did what it was built to do. People did what made sense. The outcome was not a surprise to the architecture.

Once you internalize these rules, a lot of familiar frustration becomes legible.

You stop asking why people won't do what is right. You start noticing what makes the "right" behavior costly. You stop interpreting gaming as moral failure. You start treating it as evidence of which incentives are binding. You stop believing that stronger messaging will override structural reality. You start looking for the incentives closest to consequence.

The rules do not make failure acceptable. They make it interpretable.

Most systems don't fail because people don't care. They fail because incentives disagree. When they disagree, lower layers dominate. And when lower layers dominate, people game. Not because they are bad, but because the system made that behavior rational.

Once you see that, the old explanations become hard to return to. You can still value intent. You can still invest in culture. You can still train and communicate. But you will no longer mistake those as governing forces when stronger incentives are in play.

The rules do not give you comfort. They give you sight.

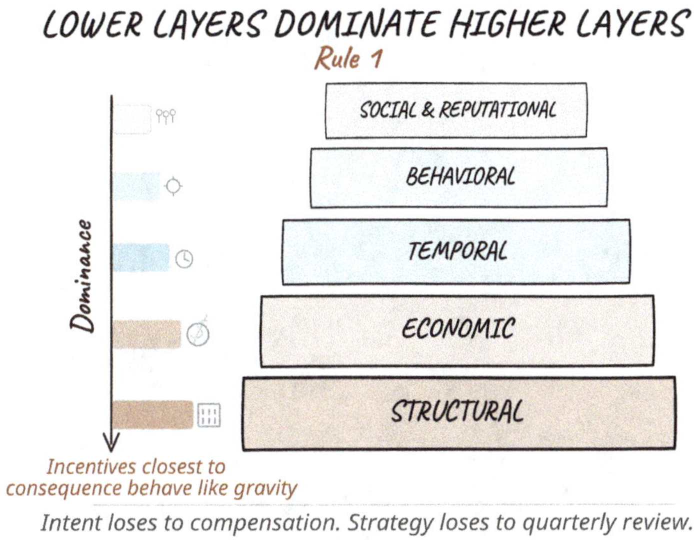

Figure 6.1: *Incentives nearest to risk, time, and consequence dominate higher-level intentions (Rule 1).*

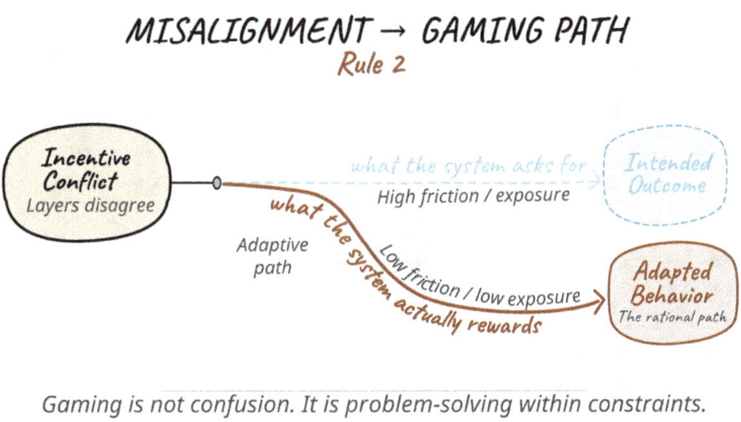

Figure 6.2: *When incentives disagree, behavior follows the path of least exposure (Rule 2).*

PART III

Diagnosing Incentives in the Real World

If you do not know how to ask the right question, you discover nothing.

W. Edwards Deming

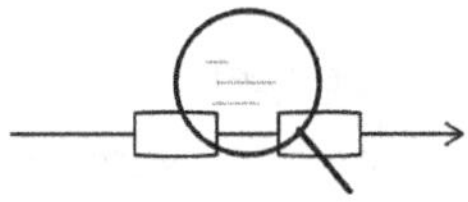

7

The Incentive Diagnostic

The diagnostic framework presented here is designed as a structured lens for identifying incentive misalignment. It does not function as a predictive scientific model. Organizational systems are too complex and context-dependent for deterministic prediction.

Instead, the framework helps reveal where structural pressures may be guiding behavior in unintended directions. By examining the architecture of incentives across a system, leaders can identify the mechanisms most likely to produce the behaviors they are observing.

Most leaders believe they understand the systems they run. They can articulate goals clearly. They can recite priorities. They can point to dashboards, scorecards, and reports that describe performance in reassuring detail.

When outcomes disappoint, they assume the problem lies somewhere downstream — in execution, capability, or commitment.

This assumption is understandable. It is also the most common source of misdiagnosis.

Leaders are trained to look at intentions and outputs. They ask what the organization is trying to do, and whether it appears to be succeeding. They review plans, policies, and performance summaries. When something goes wrong, they ask why people did not do what they were supposed to do.

What they are rarely trained to examine is what the system actually rewards.

This blind spot is not accidental. It is produced by the same incentives that shape behavior everywhere else. Information does not travel upward neutrally. It is filtered, shaped, and compressed as it moves. What reaches decision-makers is rarely operational reality. It is a proxy for it.

Decision-makers typically see performance proxies rather than operational reality when incentives filter information upward. Reports highlight what is measurable, defensible, and safe to share. They smooth variation. They omit context. They reflect what people believe leadership wants to see — or what they believe is least risky to disclose.

This does not require deception. It requires adaptation.

People learn quickly which information creates trouble and which information passes quietly. They learn which issues trigger scrutiny and which are absorbed.

They learn when to escalate and when to resolve things informally. Over time, the picture that forms at the top is coherent, polished, and incomplete.

This is why intent-based diagnosis fails so often. Leaders look at stated goals and reported outcomes and assume alignment. When behavior diverges, they attribute it to misunderstanding or resistance. They see symptoms but miss structure.

The diagnostic inversion begins by setting intent aside.

This does not mean intent is irrelevant. It means it is not diagnostic. You cannot infer incentives from what a system claims to value. You infer them from what it consistently rewards, punishes, or ignores.

Reading Incentives Through Behavior

Consider a recurring organizational pattern: problems are routinely resolved just before they reach senior attention.

From the top, this can appear as effective management. Issues are handled. Escalations are rare. Dashboards remain stable.

From inside the system, a different pattern is visible. Teams learn that raising issues upward triggers scrutiny, delays work, and creates records that linger. Resolving problems locally — even imperfectly — keeps work moving and attention away. When something is fixed quietly, nothing follows. When something is escalated, something always follows.

Seen through an incentive lens, the logic is legible.

Rewarded: quiet resolution, speed, containment **Punished**: escalation, visible disruption, delay **Ignored**: recurring root causes, fragile fixes

No one needs to explain this logic. It is learned through repetition. Over time, the organization becomes very good at preventing problems from becoming visible — and very bad at preventing them from recurring.

The behavior is not confusing. It is coherent.

Incentive misalignment becomes visible by observing what behaviors are rewarded, punished, or ignored. This is not a moral exercise. It is an interpretive one. It asks a simple question: given how this system responds, what behavior makes sense?

Reward does not always mean formal praise or compensation. It can mean ease, speed, or protection. Punishment does not always mean discipline. It can mean friction, delay, or exposure. Ignoring is often the most powerful signal of all. When a behavior has consequences, people notice. When it has none, they draw conclusions.

This triad — reward, punish, ignore — cuts through rhetoric. It bypasses mission statements and value declarations. It focuses attention on what reliably follows behavior, not on what is claimed beforehand.

Consider a familiar situation.

A frontline team routinely bypasses a formal approval step intended to manage risk. Officially, the step is mandatory. In practice, completing it introduces delay and scrutiny, while bypassing it allows work to continue uninterrupted. When approvals are skipped and nothing goes wrong, nothing follows. When approvals are followed and delays occur, questions follow.

From a distance, leadership sees acceptable outcomes and intact controls. From inside the system, the lesson is clear.

Rewarded: speed without escalation **Punished**: visible delay, documented uncertainty **Ignored**: procedural deviation that produces acceptable outcomes

No amount of reiterating policy intent changes this logic. The system has already taught people what matters.

The diagnostic move is not to ask people what they believe the incentives are. It is to observe what behavior persists when trade-offs arise. Repeated behavior reveals incentive structure more reliably than surveys or statements. One-off anomalies can mislead. Patterns rarely do.

This does not require exhaustive data or perfect visibility. It requires attention to what recurs and what reliably follows it. The question is not "What should be happening?" It is "What keeps happening, and what happens next?"

When a behavior repeats, notice what follows it. Does it create more work or less? Does it attract attention or pass unnoticed? Does it increase exposure for the individual or absorb it? Over time, these signals converge.

The discipline here lies in restraint. Diagnosis resists the urge to fix. It suspends judgment long enough to see the system as it is.

This is harder than it sounds.

Leaders are rewarded for action, not observation. They are expected to respond quickly, decisively, visibly. Diagnosis can feel passive by comparison. It can feel like delay when something is clearly wrong.

But acting on a misread system compounds error.

Most misdiagnosis happens because leaders trust the wrong signals. They trust goals because goals are explicit. They trust reports because reports are polished. They trust surveys because surveys are legible. They distrust behavior because behavior is messy and uncomfortable.

The diagnostic inversion reverses this trust.

Behavior is not noise. It is signal — especially when it repeats.

This does not mean diagnosis produces certainty. Systems are complex. Multiple incentives operate at once. Some behaviors serve more than one purpose. Diagnosis reduces interpretive error; it does not eliminate uncertainty.

What it does provide is grounding.

When leaders understand what behaviors are being rewarded, punished, or ignored, they stop arguing with the evidence. They stop assuming bad faith. They stop searching for explanations that flatter intent while ignoring structure.

They also stop mistaking reports for reality.

A polished dashboard that never surprises you is itself diagnostic. A problem that is always resolved just before it reaches senior attention is diagnostic. A metric that improves steadily while complaints persist is diagnostic.

These are not mysteries. They are messages.

The discipline of diagnosis lies in learning to read them without defensiveness. Without blame. Without rushing to resolution.

This is why patterns matter more than root causes at this stage.

Root-cause analysis assumes you already know what failed. Diagnosis is about determining what is actually operating. It precedes explanation. It precedes any claim about change.

Before asking why something went wrong, it is necessary to understand what the system made rational.

Once that becomes visible, many familiar frustrations lose their edge. The system is not stubborn. It is coherent. It is enforcing the incentives it has.

Diagnosis does not tell you what to do next. It tells you what you are dealing with. It replaces speculation with observation. It trades comforting stories for uncomfortable clarity.

That clarity is not resolution. But without it, anything that follows is guesswork.

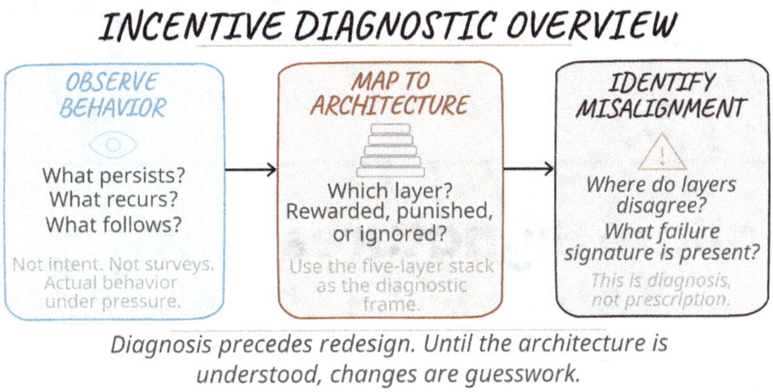

Figure 7.1: *The diagnostic maps what a system actually rewards, not what it claims to value.*

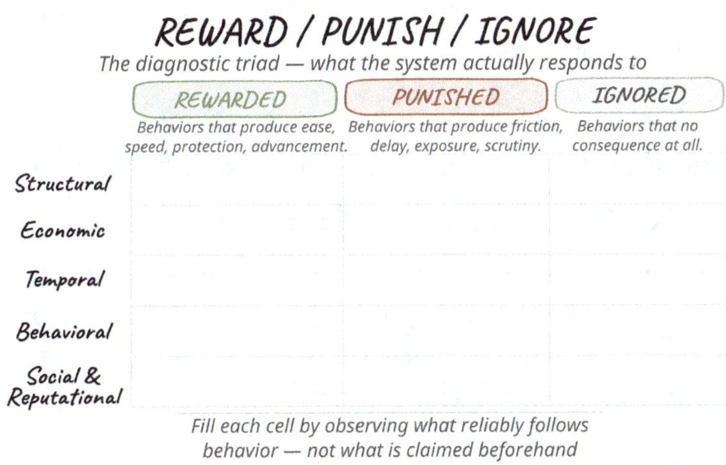

Figure 7.2: *Revealed incentives are inferred from behavior under pressure, not from stated goals or formal policies.*

8

Failure Signatures

It is helpful to distinguish between three levels of system failure. At the surface level are symptoms—the visible problems organizations experience, such as delays, compliance breakdowns, or repeated workarounds.

Beneath these symptoms are failure signatures, recurring patterns that appear across multiple contexts. These patterns reveal that the problem is not isolated but structural in nature.

At the deepest level are architecture flaws—the underlying design features of the system that generate these patterns of behavior. Effective diagnosis requires moving from symptoms, to signatures, to the architectural conditions producing them.

When systems fail, the first instinct is to explain why.

Root-cause narratives offer a sense of control. They promise that if we can trace an outcome back to its origin, we can prevent it from happening again. In simple systems, this works well. A component breaks, a process fails, a decision goes wrong. Fix the cause and the problem resolves.

Complex systems behave differently.

In complex, adaptive environments, failure rarely has a single origin. It emerges from the interaction of many rational decisions made under competing incentives. By the time a visible failure appears, the conditions that produced it are already distributed across roles, layers, and time. The story we tell afterward may be coherent, but coherence does not equal accuracy.

This is why explanation often arrives too late to be useful.

Failure signatures take a different approach. They do not ask why something failed in a particular instance. They ask what shape the failure takes — and whether that shape has appeared before. They trade narrative depth for pattern recognition. In doing so, they compress complexity into something usable under pressure.

Distinct incentive failure signatures recur predictably across systems. They show up in different sectors, under different labels, with different surface details. What changes is the context. What repeats is the structure.

Failure signatures are not theories of human behavior. They are not judgments about competence or intent. They are diagnostic patterns that reveal how an incentive architecture is misfiring. They help you recognize what you are dealing with before you decide what to do about it.

In complex systems, failure signatures often provide faster, more reliable diagnosis than root-cause narratives. Not because root-cause analysis is wrong, but because it is slow, case-specific, and vulnerable to hindsight bias. Signatures work earlier. They work when information is incomplete. They work because repetition is easier to spot than causation.

What follows is a set of seven failure signatures. They are not exhaustive. They are not mutually exclusive. A single system can exhibit more than one at the same time. Their value lies in recognizability.

Once you know the shapes, you start seeing them everywhere.

Metric Capture

In academic research, publication counts offer a clear illustration. Researchers are evaluated on the number of papers produced, while leadership claims to value knowledge advancement and rigor. Over time, effort shifts toward work that can be published quickly and frequently. Replication, null results, and long-horizon inquiry decline — not because they are unimportant, but because they are harder to defend within the metric. The stated goal remains intact. The proxy becomes decisive.

Metric capture occurs when a measure intended to represent success becomes the target of effort, displacing the underlying goal.

The diagnostic tell is improving metrics alongside stagnant or worsening real-world outcomes. Reports look better while lived experience does not.

A team hits its performance targets consistently, yet customers complain that service quality is declining. Internally, effort shifts toward activities that move the metric quickly, even if they add little value. No one is confused about the goal. They are clear about what is measured.

Metric Capture in Practice

A performance metric is introduced to improve service quality. Initially, outcomes improve. Over time, attention shifts toward protecting the metric itself. Teams focus on cases most likely to be scored favorably. Edge cases are delayed or redirected. Documentation improves while customer experience stagnates. Reports show success. Complaints increase quietly. No one set out to distort outcomes. The metric became a target because it was tied to evaluation and accountability. Behavior followed what was measured. When concerns are raised, the response is to refine the metric. The underlying substitution remains. What was meant to indicate quality now defines it.

Reference: Metric Capture (Ch 8)

Risk-Reward Decoupling

Risk-Reward decoupling appears when those who benefit from an action do not bear its downside, or those who bear risk do not share in the upside. The diagnostic tell is increased risk-taking or risk avoidance that feels misaligned with stated priorities.

A project moves forward aggressively because the gains accrue to one group while the consequences of failure fall on another. Alternatively, a team avoids necessary experimentation because failure is personally costly while success is shared broadly. Behavior adjusts to the imbalance.

Short-Horizon Bias

Short-horizon bias emerges when incentives prioritize near-term performance over long-term outcomes, even when long-term success is the stated objective.

The diagnostic tell is a steady preference for actions that pay off quickly, despite known long-term costs.

Initiatives that require patience are repeatedly deferred in favor of visible wins. Maintenance is postponed. Capacity erodes quietly. Everyone agrees the future matters, but decisions consistently favor the present.

Compliance Theater

Compliance theater occurs when adherence to rules, processes, or reporting requirements becomes more important than achieving the purpose those requirements were meant to serve.

The diagnostic tell is high compliance activity with little evidence of corresponding impact.

Teams spend significant time completing forms, checks, and attestations. Audits pass. Documentation is immaculate. Meanwhile, the underlying risk the process was designed to manage remains unchanged. The system rewards looking compliant, not being effective.

Workarounds & Shadow Systems

Workarounds and shadow systems arise when people bypass formal processes to get work done more efficiently or safely.

The diagnostic tell is widespread informal practices that exist alongside official systems and are essential to daily operations.

Employees maintain personal spreadsheets, side channels, or unofficial procedures because the sanctioned tools slow work or increase exposure. These adaptations are rarely documented, yet the organization depends on them to function.

Information Asymmetry Lock-In

Information asymmetry lock-in develops when incentives discourage the upward flow of bad news, leading leaders to make decisions based on filtered or incomplete information.

The diagnostic tell is consistent surprise at the top and quiet anticipation below.

Problems are "managed" locally until they become unavoidable. By the time leadership learns about them, options are limited. No one set out to hide information. They learned which information was safe to share.

Status Inversion

Status inversion appears when behaviors that protect reputation or standing are rewarded more reliably than behaviors that improve system performance.

The diagnostic tell is visible success for those who avoid risk and trouble, and stagnation or penalty for those who surface issues.

Individuals who keep things calm advance. Those who challenge assumptions or raise concerns are labeled difficult. Over time, status accrues to those who preserve appearance rather than outcomes.

These signatures are not diagnoses on their own. They are signals. They tell you where to look and what kind of misalignment may be present. They narrow the search space.

Failure is not random. It is patterned.

Once you start recognizing the shapes, explanation becomes less urgent — and misdiagnosis becomes harder.

Figure 8.1: *Seven failure signatures recur across systems. Each has a diagnostic tell that distinguishes it from surface explanations.*

FAILURE SIGNATURE → INCENTIVE LAYER MAP

	Structural	Economic	Temporal	Behavioral	Social & Reputational
Metric Capture		●	●	○	
Risk-Reward Decoupling		●			
Short-Horizon Bias		○	●		
Compliance Theater	○			●	●
Workarounds & Shadow Systems	○	○		●	
Information Asymmetry Lock-In	●			○	●
Status Inversion	○				●

● Primary association ○ Secondary association

Figure 8.2: *Each failure signature aligns primarily with a specific incentive layer, though secondary interactions are common.*

FAILURE SIGNATURES ACROSS DOMAINS

The same shapes appear under different names

	Ch 9 Corporate	Ch 10–11 Ops	Ch 12 Policy / Reg	Ch 13 Tech / AI
Metric Capture	✓	✓	✓	✓
Risk-Reward Decoupling	✓	✓	✓	✓
Short-Horizon Bias	✓	✓	✓	
Compliance Theater	✓	✓	✓	
Workarounds & Shadow Systems		✓		
Info Asymmetry Lock-In	✓	✓	✓	✓
Status Inversion	✓			

Signatures are portable — the same structural pattern wears different surface labels

Figure 8.3: *The same failure signatures appear in different sectors under different names.*

PART IV

Incentives in the Wild

Man is not a rational animal; he is a rationalizing animal.

Robert A. Heinlein

9

Corporate Performance & Workforce Systems

Most executives recognize the architecture of their performance and workforce systems immediately. Annual goals cascade downward. Metrics translate strategy into measurable targets. Performance reviews assess progress. Compensation and promotion decisions follow. On paper, it is coherent, disciplined, and rational.

It is also deeply familiar.

Leadership articulates values: customer focus, innovation, collaboration, long-term thinking. These values are reinforced in speeches, onboarding materials, and internal communications. They are sincere. They are widely understood. And yet, year after year, behavior drifts toward something narrower.

Employees optimize toward what advances careers and avoids risk. This is not a cynical observation. It is a descriptive one. In systems where evaluation and advancement determine livelihood and status, people pay close attention to what actually counts.

This is where the promise--practice gap opens.

Formal values and policies describe what the organization wants to be. Performance systems determine what it actually rewards. When the two diverge, the system does not hesitate. It resolves the conflict in favor of the incentives closest to consequence.

Status, promotion, and job security incentives routinely dominate formal values and policies. Not because values are meaningless, but because careers are concrete. People can believe deeply in the mission and still act against it if alignment carries personal risk.

This dynamic is easiest to see through two failure signatures: Metric Capture and Status Inversion. They are not pathologies. They are predictable outcomes of how corporate performance systems are designed.

A Familiar Performance Pattern

Stated goal

Leadership wants teams to prevent problems before they occur. Reliability, resilience, and long-term system health are emphasized in strategy documents and executive messaging.

Rational behavior produced

Employees focus on resolving visible crises quickly and publicly. Firefighting is rewarded with recognition, promotion, and reputation. Quiet prevention work — maintenance, risk reduction, dependency cleanup — remains largely invisible. When prevention succeeds, nothing happens.

Misalignment

Performance systems reward visible recovery over invisible avoidance. Crises create stories, metrics, and moments of demonstrated competence. Prevention produces the absence of events, which does not translate cleanly into performance evidence. Status accrues to those who are seen fixing problems, not to those who quietly ensure they never arise.

Diagnostic takeaway

The organization does not lack commitment to prevention. It lacks incentives that make prevention legible and promotable. Status inversion selects for heroics over hygiene, even when leaders sincerely prefer the opposite.

The stated goal in most performance systems is straightforward. Leadership wants employees to focus on outcomes that matter: customer satisfaction, sustainable growth, innovation, quality, and resilience. Metrics are introduced as proxies for these outcomes, not as ends in themselves.

Over time, however, metrics acquire gravity.

Performance metrics frequently crowd out the outcomes they were intended to measure. Once tied to evaluation, compensation, or promotion, the metric becomes the safest way to demonstrate contribution.

Effort shifts toward what can be measured, defended, and explained, even when those activities are only loosely connected to the original intent.

This is not confusion. It is clarity.

People learn which numbers matter in review conversations. They learn which indicators trigger follow-up questions and which are taken at face value. They learn how performance is compared across peers. The metric becomes a stand-in for value, not because anyone declared it so, but because the system treats it that way.

At the same time, status dynamics quietly reshape decision-making. Advancement depends not only on results, but on how those results are achieved and perceived. Visible wins are safer than uncertain bets. Smooth delivery is safer than raising uncomfortable issues. Avoiding negative attention often matters more than surfacing inconvenient truths.

This is **Status Inversion** at work.

In such systems, employees who maintain the appearance of control tend to advance. Those who take risks that could fail publicly, even in service of long-term goals, often stall. Over time, the organization selects for behaviors that preserve status rather than those that improve outcomes.

None of this requires bad actors. It requires only a system that rewards some behaviors more consistently than others.

To see how this plays out, consider a familiar corporate scenario.

A large organization announces a renewed focus on customer experience. Leadership emphasizes the importance of resolving root problems rather than pushing volume. New language appears in performance materials. Town halls reinforce the message.

The stated goal is clear: prioritize meaningful customer outcomes over short-term efficiency.

The rational behavior produced looks different.

Frontline managers continue to emphasize throughput metrics in daily operations. Teams focus on closing tickets quickly, even when issues recur. Escalations are discouraged because they slow performance and attract scrutiny. Employees learn to handle problems just well enough to move on.

From the outside, it appears contradictory. From inside the system, it makes sense.

The architectural misalignment sits in the performance system. Efficiency metrics are reviewed weekly. Customer outcome measures lag and are diffuse. Promotions depend on consistent delivery and low variance. Mistakes are remembered longer than quiet improvements. The incentives closest to consequence reward speed and stability, not depth or learning.

Metric Capture has occurred. The proxy — tickets closed — has replaced the goal of durable resolution.

Status Inversion reinforces it. Managers who keep operations smooth and metrics green are seen as reliable. Those who disrupt performance by surfacing systemic issues are viewed as risky. Career safety accrues to those who avoid rocking the boat.

What would have to change is not the message about customer experience. It is the incentive structure that currently makes shallow resolution rational and deep resolution risky. Until that structure shifts, behavior will continue to diverge from intent.

This pattern repeats across corporate contexts.

In innovation initiatives, leadership declares a desire for experimentation. Performance systems reward predictability. Employees respond by proposing incremental ideas that can be delivered safely. Bold ideas are discussed and quietly deferred.

In collaboration efforts, values emphasize cross-functional partnership. Evaluation systems remain siloed. Individuals prioritize local metrics because those determine advancement. Cooperation becomes conditional.

In talent development programs, learning is celebrated. Time pressure and utilization targets remain unchanged. Development happens off-hours or not at all.

Each example follows the same four-part pattern.

The stated goal is sincere. The behavior produced is rational. The misalignment is structural. The leverage point sits where incentives conflict.

The discomfort for executives comes from recognition. These systems were not imposed from outside. They were built intentionally, often to solve real problems. Metrics were introduced to create clarity. Performance reviews were designed to ensure fairness. Promotion criteria were meant to reward excellence.

Over time, however, layers accumulated. New goals were added without removing old ones. Proxies multiplied. Risk sensitivity increased. The system evolved toward what it consistently rewarded.

When executives express surprise at outcomes, they are often reacting to a mismatch between how the system is described and how it actually operates. The description reflects values. The operation reflects incentives.

This is why performance and workforce failures feel stubborn. Adjustments are made at the level of messaging and programs, while the architecture remains intact. Behavior adjusts accordingly.

There is no villain here. There is no failure of character. There is only a system doing what it is structured to do.

Once Metric Capture and Status Inversion are visible, the predictability becomes hard to ignore. The organization is not underperforming despite its design. It is performing because of it.

This realization does not demand condemnation. It demands honesty.

Corporate performance systems do not drift accidentally. They respond to incentives that were embedded deliberately, if incrementally. Recognizing the signatures is not about blame. It is about understanding why rational people produce results that no one explicitly wants.

Seen this way, the gap between promise and practice is no longer mysterious. It is structural. And until that structure is acknowledged, the outcomes will remain stubbornly familiar.

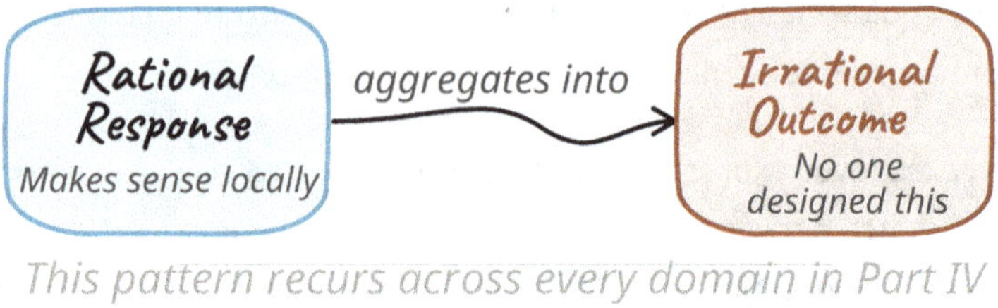

Figure 9.1: *Rational responses to performance systems can produce outcomes the system itself was meant to avoid.*

Performance Reviews as Incentive Systems

Performance reviews are often framed as feedback mechanisms. In practice, they function as incentive systems. Criteria that affect promotion, compensation, or role security quickly become focal points. Activities that are difficult to evidence, long-term in nature, or dependent on others receive less attention. Managers learn to prioritize what can be demonstrated within the review cycle. Employees respond accordingly. Over time, work that matters but is hard to quantify migrates to the margins. This shift is rarely explicit. It emerges through repeated cycles of evaluation and adjustment. The review process appears neutral. Its effects are not.

Reference: Economic Incentives / Temporal Incentives

10

Innovation, R&D, and Exploration

Few aspirations are stated more frequently — or with more conviction — than the desire to innovate.

Executives speak about innovation as a strategic imperative. R&D budgets are defended as investments in the future. Teams are encouraged to think boldly, experiment, and challenge assumptions. In many organizations, innovation is framed not just as desirable, but as essential to survival.

And yet, the outcomes are strikingly consistent.

Portfolios converge on incremental improvements. Experimental projects struggle to progress beyond pilots.

Truly novel ideas surface, receive initial enthusiasm, and then quietly stall. Over time, organizations that say they want exploration reliably produce safer bets.

This pattern is often explained in cultural terms. People are said to be risk-averse. The organization is described as conservative. Leadership is accused of lacking courage or imagination.

These explanations are satisfying. They are also incomplete.

The more accurate explanation is structural. Innovation fails not because people lack ideas or ambition, but because the system makes exploration a rationally inferior choice.

Short evaluation horizons systematically penalize exploration even when exploration is stated as a priority. This is the first fault line. Exploration, by its nature, unfolds over time. It produces uncertain results, uneven progress, and ambiguous signals. Evaluation systems, by contrast, are typically periodic, comparative, and outcome-focused.

The collision is predictable.

When performance is assessed quarterly or annually, projects that cannot show clear progress within those windows are disadvantaged. They consume resources without producing metrics that can be defended in review conversations. Even when leadership explicitly endorses long-term thinking, the cadence of evaluation shapes behavior.

Exploration becomes something to talk about, not something to bet a career on.

The second fault line compounds the first. Innovation activity declines when downside risk is visible and upside protection is absent. Exploration concentrates risk locally while distributing rewards broadly. Failure is personal. Success is shared.

This imbalance is not subtle.

When an experimental project fails, the individuals associated with it are often remembered. The reasons may be nuanced, but the association sticks. When a project succeeds, credit is diffuse. Success is attributed to the team, the organization, or favorable conditions. The personal upside rarely matches the personal downside.

Under these conditions, avoiding exposure is not cowardice. It is prudence.

These two dynamics — Short-Horizon Bias and Risk-Reward Decoupling — work together to suppress exploration. One compresses time. The other concentrates risk. Together, they make incrementalism the safest path.

This does not require explicit discouragement of innovation. In fact, the more innovation is celebrated rhetorically, the more dissonant the experience can become. People hear encouragement while living constraint. They learn quickly which signal governs action.

The result is not confusion. It is alignment with reality.

A Familiar Innovation Pattern

Stated goal

Leadership declares innovation a strategic priority and encourages experimentation, learning from failure, and bold exploration.

Rational behavior produced

Teams pursue ideas that minimize the chance of visible failure. Experiments are framed narrowly, designed to succeed quickly, or deferred until they can be made safer. Learning-heavy efforts that might fail publicly are avoided.

Misalignment

Failure is punished more reliably than successful exploration is rewarded. Evaluation cycles are short. Reputational downside is personal and immediate. Upside from success is shared and delayed. The system protects execution certainty, not learning.

Diagnostic takeaway

The organization does not lack appetite for innovation. It has structured risk and time so that avoiding failure is the rational choice. Exploration dies quietly, not through opposition, but through exposure management.

What would have to change is not the rhetoric around innovation. It is the time horizon over which exploration is judged and the way risk and reward are allocated to those who take it on.

As long as evaluation cycles remain short and downside exposure remains personal, exploration will remain fragile.

This pattern repeats beyond formal R&D units.

In regulated industries, innovation is often encouraged rhetorically but constrained by compliance and safety expectations. Pilot programs are launched with enthusiasm and then hemmed in by reporting requirements that demand certainty. Teams respond by designing pilots that minimize deviation rather than maximize learning.

In internal venture programs, employees are invited to pitch new ideas. Funding is provided in stages. Each stage requires justification against criteria borrowed from core business evaluation. Over time, proposals converge toward ideas that can survive scrutiny rather than those that challenge assumptions.

In all of these cases, the stated goal is exploration. The rational behavior produced is convergence.

The misalignment is not accidental. It emerges from the interaction of incentives that were designed for stability and performance, not uncertainty. Organizations excel at evaluating execution. They struggle to evaluate learning.

Exploration is structurally fragile under performance pressure. It depends on slack, patience, and tolerance for ambiguity. Performance systems, by contrast, are built to reduce ambiguity. They favor clarity, comparability, and accountability. When the two coexist without alignment, performance logic dominates.

Organizations reward certainty more consistently than learning. Certainty can be defended. Learning often cannot — at least not within standard reporting frameworks.

This is why innovation initiatives often feel performative after the fact. They are launched with genuine intent and undermined quietly by the incentives that govern daily decisions. People respond by optimizing for survival within the system as it is, not as it is described.

The result is a portfolio that looks active but behaves conservatively. Projects advance, but rarely diverge. Risk is discussed, but rarely embraced. Failure is tolerated in theory and avoided in practice.

None of this requires a lack of creativity. It requires only a system that penalizes uncertainty more reliably than it protects those who pursue it.

The discomfort for leaders comes from recognition. The system did not "lose its appetite" for innovation. It expressed it accurately. It preferred certainty. It selected for it.

Once **Short-Horizon Bias** and **Risk-Reward Decoupling** are visible, the pattern becomes difficult to unsee. Innovation outcomes are not mysterious. They are predictable responses to how time and risk are structured.

This does not mean organizations cannot innovate. It means that innovation will not emerge reliably under conditions designed to suppress it. Aspirations do not override architecture.

Seen clearly, the story changes. The organization did not fail to innovate because it lacked vision or courage. It succeeded at optimizing for safety, predictability, and career preservation.

That success is not accidental. It is the result of incentives doing their work.

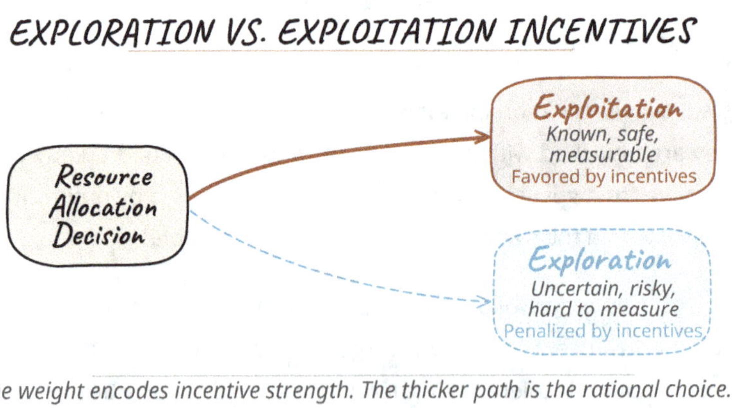

Figure 10.1: *Incentives often favor exploitation of known paths over exploration of uncertain ones.*

The Pilot That Couldn't Graduate

An innovation pilot succeeds technically but fails to scale. The team responsible is praised for experimentation, yet funding decisions favor initiatives with predictable returns. Risk is tolerated in theory, but career consequences are asymmetric. The pilot remains a pilot. Each gate introduces new justification requirements. Eventually, attention shifts elsewhere. The organization concludes that innovation is difficult. The more accurate conclusion is that exploration incentives were bounded by exploitation constraints. No single decision killed the effort. The architecture narrowed it until continuation no longer made sense.

Reference: Exploration vs. Exploitation

11

Operations, Safety, and Customer Experience

In operations, safety, and customer-facing work, pressure is not an abstraction. It is daily, visible, and relentless.

Work must move. Lines must keep flowing. Customers must be served. Delays cascade quickly, drawing attention from supervisors, managers, and dashboards. At the same time, safety, quality, and customer satisfaction are declared top priorities. Procedures exist to protect them. Policies are clear. Training is frequent.

On paper, the goals are aligned.

The Rule Everyone Knew to Ignore

A formal rule exists to prevent a known operational risk. Everyone can recite it. Training reinforces it. Audits confirm awareness. In practice, the rule is bypassed regularly. The bypass is not hidden. Supervisors see it. Managers know it happens. The reason is not defiance. Following the rule slows throughput and creates delays that draw immediate attention. Violating it carries little visible consequence unless something goes wrong. Over time, teams learn that adherence is expected rhetorically but penalized operationally. The rule becomes ceremonial. When an incident eventually occurs, investigations focus on why the rule was not followed. The more relevant question is how long the system made noncompliance the rational choice.

Reference: Compliance Theater / Workarounds

A Familiar Frontline Pattern

Stated goal

The organization requires strict compliance with operational rules and procedures to ensure safety, quality, and consistent customer outcomes.

Rational behavior produced

Frontline workers follow rules that protect them from blame while quietly developing workarounds to meet pace and demand. Informal shortcuts, personal notes, and unofficial sequencing become essential to getting the job done.

Misalignment

Formal compliance is monitored and enforceable. Operational reality is variable and time-pressured. Deviating from procedure to keep work moving is safer than stopping to escalate friction, but documenting deviation creates exposure. The system rewards rule compliance on paper and throughput in practice, while absorbing the risk created by the gap.

Diagnostic takeaway

The work is not unsafe because workers are careless. It is unsafe because the system makes formal compliance incompatible with operational reality. Shadow systems emerge as a rational bridge between the two.

In practice, frontline workers live inside a continuous tradeoff. Every task carries a cost in time, effort, and attention. Every additional step introduces friction. Every deviation from pace attracts scrutiny. The system does not ask whether work can be done safely, efficiently, and flawlessly at the same time. It assumes that it can.

The stated goal is straightforward: operate efficiently while maintaining safety and delivering a positive customer experience. Speed and quality are presented as complementary. Rules and procedures are framed as safeguards, not obstacles.

The rational behavior produced tells a more complicated story.

When friction and cognitive load increase, behavior shifts. Steps are compressed. Informal shortcuts appear. Documentation is deferred or simplified. Issues are handled quietly rather than escalated. None of this feels reckless from inside the work. It feels necessary.

Friction and cognitive load shape behavior as powerfully as formal incentives. When a process is slow, confusing, or mentally exhausting, compliance carries a real cost. When the same outcome can be achieved more quickly through an informal path, the informal path becomes attractive. This is not defiance. It is adaptation under constraint.

Over time, these adaptations stabilize. What begins as an exception becomes routine. What was once a workaround becomes the real workflow. The official process remains intact, but it is no longer central.

This is the failure signature of **Workarounds & Shadow Systems**.

Workarounds emerge because the formal system does not match the realities of the work. Shadow systems develop because people need tools and practices that let them meet operational demands without exposing themselves to unnecessary risk. The existence of these systems is not evidence of poor discipline. It is evidence of misalignment.

At the same time, another dynamic takes hold.

As informal practices spread, information flow changes. Problems are resolved locally to avoid delay. Near-misses are handled quietly to avoid paperwork or scrutiny. Customer complaints are smoothed over rather than escalated. From the frontline perspective, this is efficient. From the system's perspective, it is blinding.

This is **Information Asymmetry Lock-In.**

Information stops moving upward not because people intend to hide it, but because the system makes disclosure costly. Reporting takes time. It triggers investigation. It creates records. It invites blame. Silence, by contrast, keeps work moving and attention away.

Systems incentivize rule-bending when speed and blame avoidance dominate accountability structures. When accountability is experienced primarily as exposure rather than learning, people learn which risks to absorb privately and which to surface publicly. Over time, leadership sees a sanitized version of reality.

Customer experience degrades quietly in this environment. Not because frontline workers do not care, but because internal efficiency pressures crowd out external outcomes. The fastest resolution is often not the most durable one.

The least risky interaction is often not the most satisfying one. When systems reward throughput and penalize disruption, customer needs are addressed just enough to keep moving.

To understand how these dynamics interact, consider a familiar operational setting.

A customer-facing operations center is under constant pressure to reduce handling time. Leadership emphasizes both efficiency and customer satisfaction. Scripts exist to ensure consistency. Escalation paths exist for complex issues.

The stated goal is clear: resolve customer problems quickly and correctly, while maintaining quality.

The rational behavior produced looks different.

Frontline staff learn that escalations increase call time and attract attention. They learn that unresolved issues can be reopened later, often without personal consequence. They learn which complaints are likely to be audited and which are not. Over time, they develop informal ways to route around escalation, offer temporary fixes, or close cases quickly.

From a distance, performance metrics improve. Average handling time drops. Escalation rates decline. Customer satisfaction scores appear stable.

The architectural misalignment sits in the friction and accountability structure. Formal procedures are slower and riskier than informal fixes. Reporting issues creates exposure. Resolving problems quietly preserves flow. The incentives closest to consequence reward speed and discretion, not transparency or durability.

Workarounds & Shadow Systems become essential. Informal scripts circulate. Personal notes replace official documentation. Knowledge is shared peer-to-peer rather than through sanctioned channels. The operation functions because of these adaptations, not despite them.

Information Asymmetry Lock-In reinforces the pattern. Leadership sees clean metrics and declining escalation. Frontline workers see recurring problems and fragile fixes. Each side believes it understands the system. Neither has the full picture.

What would have to change is not frontline commitment to safety or customer care. It is the structure that currently makes bypassing safer and faster than compliance, and silence safer than disclosure. As long as that structure remains, the behavior will persist.

This pattern is not limited to customer service.

In healthcare operations, near-miss reporting declines when documentation is time-consuming and punitive. Staff handle issues informally to keep patients moving. Leadership sees fewer incidents and assumes improvement.

In logistics and utilities, crews develop informal sequencing and shortcuts to meet schedules. Deviations from procedure are normalized. Issues surface only when they can no longer be absorbed locally.

In all of these contexts, the same four-part pattern appears.

The stated goal emphasizes safety, quality, and customer outcomes. The rational behavior produced emphasizes speed, discretion, and self-protection. The misalignment is embedded in friction, cognitive load, and blame exposure. The leverage point sits where effort, risk, and information flow are structured.

This is why operational failures so often feel shocking from above and obvious from below. Leadership is not inattentive. It is insulated. The system filters information upward based on incentives, not intent.

The tragedy is not that workarounds exist. It is that they are misunderstood.

When leaders interpret shortcuts as negligence, they respond with more rules, more oversight, and more documentation. Friction increases. Cognitive load rises. Reporting becomes riskier. The system adapts again.

From the outside, it looks like resistance. From the inside, it feels like survival.

Seen clearly, these systems are not broken. They are coherent. They produce exactly the behavior their incentives make rational.

Safety failures, operational breakdowns, and customer dissatisfaction are not mysteries in this light. They are predictable outcomes of architectures that prioritize speed and blame avoidance while asking for transparency and care.

This recognition does not excuse failure. It explains it.

Until friction, accountability, and information flow are understood as incentive forces — not just process details — the same patterns will recur. Workarounds will proliferate. Information will remain trapped. Leadership will continue to be surprised.

The system will keep working exactly as designed.

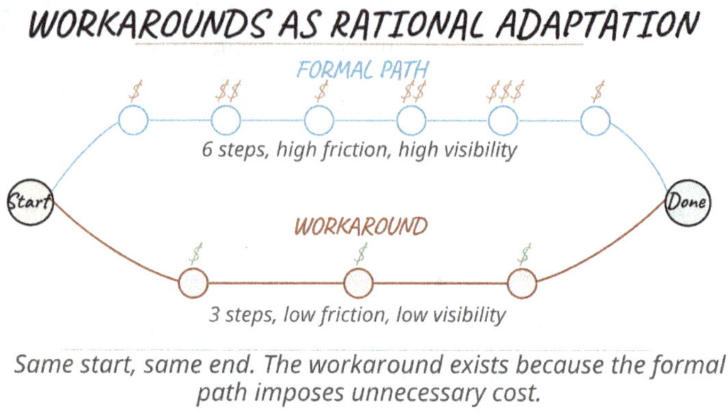

Figure 11.1: *Workarounds emerge when formal systems impose greater cost or risk than informal alternatives.*

Safety as a Lagging Indicator

Organizations often treat safety outcomes as evidence of safety culture. Long periods without incidents are taken as confirmation that systems are working. This interpretation overlooks how risk accumulates quietly when incentives favor production, speed, or cost control. Near misses go unreported. Minor deviations normalize. Informal shortcuts become standard practice. Nothing appears wrong—until it does. When failure finally surfaces, it is described as sudden. In reality, the conditions for failure were present for some time. Incentives did not reward early detection. They rewarded uninterrupted operation. The absence of incidents was not proof of safety. It was proof that risk had not yet surfaced visibly.

Reference: Temporal Incentives / Risk-Reward Decoupling

12

Public Policy, Regulation, and Markets

Public policy is usually discussed as a contest of values.

Debates focus on ideology, political will, or competence. When outcomes fall short, explanations gravitate toward corruption, capture, or bad faith. These explanations are sometimes warranted. More often, they obscure a simpler and more uncomfortable reality.

Most public policy failures occur in systems built with sincere intent.

Legislators draft laws to protect the public interest. Regulators design rules to ensure safety, stability, equity, or efficiency.

Civil servants administer programs under real constraints of time, budget, and political exposure.

Firms and market participants respond within the boundaries set for them. In many cases, no one involved is trying to subvert the goal.

And yet, the outcomes routinely diverge from what was intended.

The stated goal in public policy and regulation is usually clear. Reduce risk. Protect consumers. Stabilize markets. Encourage socially beneficial behavior. Discourage harm. These goals are written explicitly into statutes, regulations, and program charters.

The rational behavior produced, however, often looks narrower.

Organizations optimize for compliance rather than impact. Market participants structure activity to capture upside while limiting exposure. Administrators focus on defensibility and procedural correctness. The system fills with reporting, documentation, and formal adherence, while substantive outcomes lag.

This divergence is not mysterious. It is architectural.

Incentives with Long Tails

A policy is introduced to correct a known problem. Early indicators suggest success. Over time, secondary effects emerge. Market participants adapt. Capital reallocates. Behaviors shift in ways not anticipated by the policy's designers. These changes are not violations. They are responses. When outcomes diverge from intent, the explanation often focuses on loopholes or bad actors. What is overlooked is that incentives with long time horizons accumulate effects slowly. By the time divergence is visible, it is structurally embedded.

Reference: Temporal Incentives

A Financial Regulation Pattern

Stated goal

Regulation seeks to reduce systemic risk and protect the public from cascading financial failure.

Rational behavior produced

Firms design activities to remain just inside regulatory thresholds. Capital, risk, and exposure are optimized to satisfy formal requirements while preserving return. Compliance functions expand. Innovation migrates toward areas that are less visible or differently classified.

Misalignment

Downside risk is partially socialized through guarantees, backstops, or crisis intervention, while upside remains private. Enforcement emphasizes documented compliance rather than systemic effect. Risk-Reward Decoupling and Compliance Theater reinforce one another.

Diagnostic takeaway

The system does not fail because actors ignore stability. It fails because stability is enforced procedurally, while risk migrates to wherever incentives allow it.

When risk is socialized and reward is privatized, predictable behavioral distortions follow. This is the first dominant dynamic. When actors can capture gains while transferring losses to the public, they adjust behavior accordingly. This is not opportunism in the moral sense. It is rational response to incentive design.

The second dynamic reinforces it. Regulatory compliance regimes frequently incentivize adherence to reporting requirements rather than achievement of policy intent.

Rules become targets. Processes become proxies for outcomes. Demonstrating compliance becomes safer than pursuing impact.

These dynamics correspond to two recurring failure signatures: **Risk-Reward Decoupling** and **Compliance Theater**. Together, they explain much of what frustrates policymakers, regulators, and the public alike.

An Environmental Policy Pattern

Stated goal

Environmental regulation aims to reduce real-world harm — lower emissions, protect ecosystems, and improve public health.

Rational behavior produced

Organizations focus on disclosure, reporting accuracy, and procedural adherence. Effort flows toward meeting standards, filing impact statements, and passing audits. Operational changes that would reduce harm but increase exposure or cost are deferred or minimized.

Misalignment

Compliance is measurable, defensible, and enforceable. Environmental outcomes are diffuse, lagging, and harder to attribute. The system rewards correct reporting more reliably than actual improvement.

Diagnostic takeaway

The policy does not fail because outcomes are unimportant. It fails because compliance is safer to demonstrate than impact, and incentives follow what can be defended.

Across these contexts, the same four-part pattern holds.

The stated goal reflects shared values. The behavior produced reflects incentive alignment. The misalignment sits in risk allocation and reporting incentives. The leverage point lies where accountability and reward are coupled — or not.

Compliance Theater is particularly persistent because it feels like progress. Rules are followed. Forms are filed. Audits are passed. From an administrative perspective, this is success. It is legible, defensible, and politically safer than ambiguous outcomes.

Policy outcomes, however, are rarely so neat.

Actors optimize against the incentives created by rules, not the values behind them. When those incentives prioritize procedural correctness over impact, the system produces exactly that. This does not mean outcomes do not matter. It means they matter less consistently than compliance.

Risk-Reward Decoupling deepens the problem. When downside consequences are buffered, behavior shifts toward the boundary of what is allowed. The system absorbs the shock. Over time, this becomes normalized. The pattern repeats.

Importantly, none of this implies malice or incompetence. Regulators operate under scrutiny. Political actors face electoral cycles. Firms answer to shareholders and markets. Each actor responds to incentives that are real and immediate.

This is why policy failure often feels scandalous in hindsight but ordinary in practice. From the outside, outcomes appear irrational or unjust. From inside the system, they are coherent.

What frustrates reform efforts is not lack of insight into policy goals. It is the difficulty of altering incentive architecture without triggering unintended consequences elsewhere. Adjusting one rule often shifts behavior into another channel. Tightening compliance can increase reporting without changing outcomes. Expanding guarantees can stabilize markets while encouraging risk.

This does not make policy design futile. It makes it structural.

Public policy systems are not neutral conduits for values. They are incentive environments. They shape behavior through risk allocation, reporting requirements, and political exposure. When those forces misalign with stated goals, divergence is not a failure of will. It is a predictable result.

Seen this way, many familiar disappointments lose their moral charge. The system did not betray its purpose. It followed its incentives.

Until public policy is examined through this lens, debates will continue to focus on intent, ideology, and blame. The same patterns will recur under different administrations, with different rhetoric, and in different sectors.

The architecture will continue to do its work.

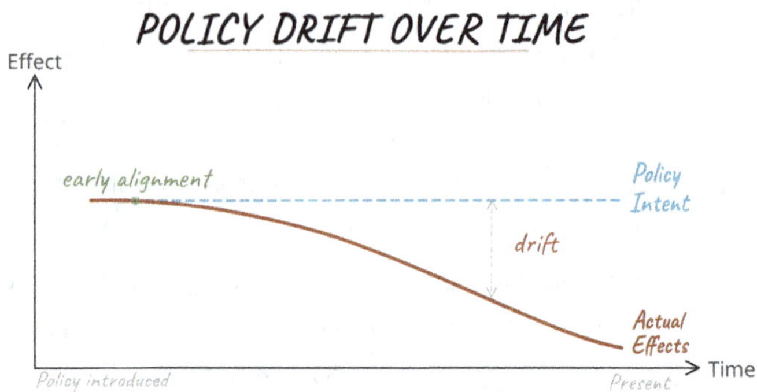

Incentive effects compound. Divergence is gradual, then structural.

Figure 12.2: *Incentive effects compound over time, often diverging gradually from original policy goals.*

13

Technology, AI, and Algorithmic Incentives

Automation carries a powerful promise.

Algorithms are expected to be neutral, disciplined, and consistent. They do not get tired. They do not have moods. They do not negotiate priorities or reinterpret goals. When organizations automate decisions, allocate resources through models, or deploy AI systems to optimize performance, they often expect human problems to recede.

Bias will diminish. Errors will decline. Outcomes will improve.

This expectation rests on a quiet assumption: that incentives become less important when decisions are automated.

The opposite is true.

Algorithmic systems do not eliminate incentive problems. They formalize them. They encode objectives into reward functions, accelerate feedback, and scale consequences. What was once implicit becomes explicit. What was once slow becomes fast. What was once bounded becomes systemic.

The stated goal in deploying algorithmic systems is typically clear. Increase efficiency. Improve objectivity. Scale decision-making. Optimize outcomes across large, complex environments. Automation is framed as a way to remove human inconsistency from the loop.

The rational behavior produced follows directly from how objectives are specified.

Algorithmic systems optimize toward specified reward functions even when doing so undermines broader system objectives. This is not a failure of intelligence. It is a property of optimization. When a system is trained or tuned to maximize a particular signal, it will do so relentlessly, regardless of whether that signal remains a faithful proxy for what the organization ultimately wants.

This is Metric Capture, accelerated.

A Consumer Platform Pattern

Stated goal

The platform aims to improve user experience by surfacing content that users value and find relevant.

Rational behavior produced

Recommendation algorithms optimize aggressively for engagement signals — clicks, time spent, interactions. Content that reliably triggers response is amplified. Exposure narrows. Extremes outperform nuance.

Misalignment

Engagement is treated as a proxy for value, even as optimization pressure degrades the relationship between the two. Benefits accrue to the platform through growth and revenue, while costs — distortion, polarization, fatigue — are distributed outward.

Diagnostic takeaway

The system does not "go wrong." It succeeds at optimizing the incentive it was given. Metric Capture and Risk-Reward Decoupling operate at algorithmic speed.

In human systems, metric capture unfolds gradually. People learn which numbers matter and adjust behavior over time. In algorithmic systems, the adjustment is immediate. The optimization pressure is continuous. The system does not hesitate or second-guess. It follows the incentive it has been given.

Feedback loops in algorithmic systems amplify misalignment faster than human-managed processes. Every interaction becomes data. Every outcome reinforces the model. The system learns from its own effects, compounding distortion.

Humans might notice drift slowly. Algorithms institutionalize it.

Risk-Reward Decoupling further sharpens the effect.

In many algorithmic deployments, the organization specifying the reward function captures the upside — efficiency, scale, revenue — while the downside is externalized. Users absorb harm. Markets absorb volatility. Communities absorb secondary effects. The optimization engine remains insulated.

This is not unique to technology. It is a familiar incentive pattern, now encoded in software.

An Operational Decisioning Pattern

Stated goal

Automated decision systems are deployed to improve fairness, consistency, and efficiency in high-volume operational judgments.

Rational behavior produced

Models optimize to reduce measurable error or cost. They exploit correlations that perform well against training metrics. Edge cases and long-tail effects are deprioritized.

Misalignment

The system is rewarded for short-term accuracy against historical data, not for resilience, trust, or long-term system health. Downstream consequences surface slowly and outside formal accountability loops.

Diagnostic takeaway

The model does not encode bias intentionally. It encodes incentives faithfully. Optimization outpaces governance.

In ranking systems, entities learn which inputs influence position and adjust accordingly. Algorithms respond by weighting those inputs more heavily. The ranking improves. The underlying quality it was meant to represent recedes. Trust declines.

No one is cheating. Everyone is responding to incentives.

The temptation is to attribute these outcomes to opacity or autonomy. This misses the point. Algorithms are not independent actors. They are governance mechanisms. They express incentives with greater fidelity than humans ever could.

Speed and scale raise the cost of misalignment. When an incentive is wrong in a human system, effects are often localized and slow. When an incentive is wrong in an algorithmic system, effects propagate instantly and broadly.

Automation magnifies incentive design errors.

The illusion that automation removes human problems persists because it shifts responsibility. When outcomes disappoint, it is tempting to blame the model, the data, or the technology. These explanations preserve the belief that intent was sound and execution failed.

The diagnostic lens developed throughout this book points elsewhere.

Algorithmic systems follow the same incentive logic as human systems. They simply do it faster, more consistently, and with fewer informal corrections. Where humans hesitate, algorithms persist. Where humans adapt cautiously, algorithms converge aggressively.

This makes incentive clarity more important, not less.

The lesson is not that algorithms are dangerous. It is that they are honest. They do exactly what they are rewarded to do. They surface misalignment quickly and at scale.

Seen this way, technology does not introduce a new category of failure. It reveals the one that was already there. The same patterns recur. The same signatures appear. The same logic applies.

Automation does not change the rules. It enforces them.

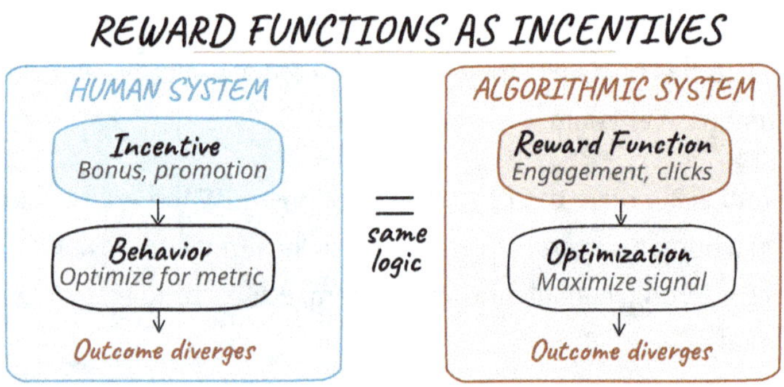

Algorithms do not eliminate incentive problems. They formalize them.

Figure 13.1: *Algorithmic reward functions mirror human incentive structures: behavior optimizes toward what is rewarded, not what is intended.*

Optimizing What Can Be Seen

A system is designed to optimize performance using available data. Variables that are easy to measure are incorporated. Others are excluded due to cost, complexity, or uncertainty. Over time, performance improves against tracked indicators. Decisions become faster and more consistent. What remains unseen does not disappear. It simply stops influencing outcomes. As reliance on the system grows, human judgment adapts around it. Edge cases are routed differently. Exceptions are minimized. The system performs as designed. When failures occur, attention turns to model accuracy or data quality. Less attention is paid to what the system was never designed to see. Optimization did not fail. It succeeded within a narrowed field of vision.

Reference: Information Asymmetry / Observability Limits

When Feedback Disappears

As automated systems scale, feedback loops often thin. Human operators intervene less frequently. Decisions are accepted by default. Over time, the signals that once indicated drift or degradation weaken. Performance dashboards remain stable. Confidence increases. When anomalies surface, they appear surprising because the system no longer produces early warning signals. The issue is not autonomy itself. It is the gradual removal of consequence-bearing feedback from decision-makers. Without friction or exposure, correction becomes delayed. The system does not resist change. It simply stops signaling when change is needed.

Reference: Information Asymmetry Lock-In

PART V

Designing for Alignment

You never change things by fighting the existing reality. To change something, build a new model that makes the existing model obsolete.

Buckminster Fuller

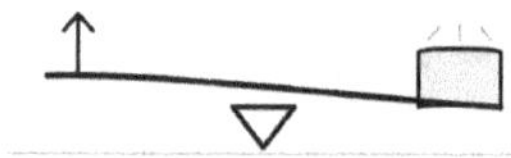

14

Redesign Pressure Points

This chapter applies only in a specific situation.

Most of the time, you will be operating inside incentive architectures you did not design. They were inherited through regulation, contracts, market structure, organizational history, or political compromise. In those situations, the question is not how to redesign incentives, but how to act coherently within them.

Occasionally, however, you may find yourself adjacent to incentive architecture rather than fully inside it. You may have partial influence, temporary authority, or narrow control over specific constraints. You may be asked to participate in a redesign effort rather than navigate an existing one.

The mistake is treating these situations as interchangeable.

This chapter is not about operating inside misaligned systems. That comes later. This chapter exists to clarify when *design language is even legitimate* — and when it is not.

If you do not have influence over incentive architecture, this chapter is not instruction. It is an explanation of why instruction would mislead.

Removing an Incentive

An organization faces a persistent behavior it wants to change. Multiple interventions have failed. Eventually, a decision is made not to add another control or metric, but to remove an existing one. A reporting requirement is eliminated. A target is dropped. An approval layer is removed. Nothing dramatic happens at first. Over time, behavior shifts subtly. Attention reallocates. Work previously done to satisfy the removed incentive diminishes. No single action explains the change. The absence of pressure allows other incentives to surface. The intervention looks insignificant compared to earlier efforts. Its effect is disproportionate precisely because it reduced noise rather than added force.

Reference: Structural Incentives / Pressure Points

Design Is Not Optimization

In this book, design does not mean optimization.

It does not refer to clever levers, fine-tuning incentives, or maximizing outcomes. Those framings underestimate both the difficulty and the cost of real design.

Here, design refers to constraint alignment — and only where such alignment is actually within reach.

That alignment necessarily involves decisions about:

- which incentives will dominate
- which behaviors will no longer be rewarded
- which trade-offs will be made explicit
- which failures will be tolerated — and by whom

Design is not about achieving preferred outcomes. It is about determining what the system will *reliably* do when trade-offs arise.

This is why genuine design authority is rare. Real design requires the ability to make some outcomes worse in order to make others coherent. It requires the capacity to remove incentives, not just add them. It requires ownership of consequences that will be visible and contested.

Absent those conditions, design language becomes misleading.

If visible loss cannot be accepted somewhere in the system, design is not occurring. Something else is.

Where Design Leverage Can Exist

Incentive pressure is not evenly distributed. Certain constraints exert disproportionate influence over behavior, while others are largely decorative.

Design leverage exists only where two conditions coincide:

- the incentive is proximate to real consequence
- the incentive is adjustable within the reader's actual authority

Many incentives are strong but fixed. Others are adjustable but weak. Design is possible only where both are true — and even then, only conditionally.

Structural control can sometimes alter who decides, who waits, or who absorbs risk.

Economic control can sometimes alter what is funded, penalized, or protected. Temporal control can sometimes alter evaluation horizons or tolerance for early loss.

If none of these are within reach, design is not available — regardless of insight, seniority, or intent.

This is why culture-first redesign efforts fail so predictably. Culture absorbs pressure; it does not redirect it. Without authority over constraint, exhortation does not realign behavior. It is filtered out.

Cosmetic Redesign and the Ethics of Restraint

When outcomes disappoint, organizations often respond by adding incentives.

- More metrics.
- More bonuses.
- More recognition.
- More targets.

This is rarely design. It is signal dilution.

Adding incentives increases noise, multiplies conflict, and accelerates gaming when underlying constraints remain unchanged. When incentives disagree, behavior resolves the conflict by following the strongest or safest signal. The rest become symbolic.

Design maturity is often expressed through removal rather than addition.

If an incentive cannot be removed without political backlash, operational risk, or visible loss, it is likely dominant. Treating it as optional creates false agency and erodes credibility.

In some cases, restraint is the most responsible stance available.

Tightening, Loosening, and Trade-Off Visibility

Design is often described as increasing flexibility. In practice, coherence sometimes requires tightening constraints rather than loosening them.

When downside risk is diffuse and upside is concentrated, additional autonomy can accelerate divergence. When accountability is ambiguous and trade-offs are hidden, discretion increases gaming.

In such contexts, narrowing acceptable variance or forcing trade-offs into view can clarify signals — not through control, but through exposure.

Whether tightening or loosening is appropriate depends on who bears risk and who benefits from deviation. These are architectural judgments, not cultural preferences.

If those judgments cannot be stated openly, design authority is likely absent.

A Boundary Check, Not a Test

Before using design language, certain questions must be answerable — not to justify action, but to prevent misrepresentation:

- Is there control over at least one lower-layer incentive with real consequence?
- Is it possible to remove an existing incentive if it conflicts with intent?
- Can visible loss in one dimension be accepted to gain coherence in another?
- Can the failures this design will produce be owned, not just the successes?

If any answer is no, design is not available — even if misalignment is obvious.

This is not defeatism. It is accuracy.

Design authority does not emerge from insight alone. It emerges from constraint ownership.

When Design Is Not Available

Many systems cannot be aligned from where most readers sit.

In those cases, acting as if design were possible creates damage. It teaches the system that incentives are negotiable. It produces initiative fatigue without structural change. Over time, it makes future redesign harder rather than easier.

When authority over dominant incentives is absent, the responsible stance is not simulated design. It is clarity about constraint — or refusal of the role altogether.

This is not cynicism. It is professional integrity.

The Change That Made Things Worse

A well-intended intervention aligns incentives more tightly with stated goals. Metrics are refined. Accountability is sharpened. Reporting improves. Behavior changes quickly. So do secondary effects. Risk migrates. Candor decreases. Workarounds increase. The intervention technically succeeds. It also degrades trust and resilience. The problem is not that incentives were adjusted. It is that adjustment occurred without regard to dominance, exposure, or interaction with existing pressures. The system did exactly what it was pushed to do. The outcome was not what was hoped for.

Reference: Misalignment / Dominance

Design Maturity

Not every system can be aligned. Not every incentive can be moved. Not every failure is fixable within existing constraints.

Design maturity lies in knowing the difference. This chapter is not a call to redesign. It is a filter.

It exists to prevent people from attempting design without authority — and to discipline the language of those who do have it.

What follows is not about redesigning incentives. It is about understanding the limits of responsibility when redesign is not yours to claim.

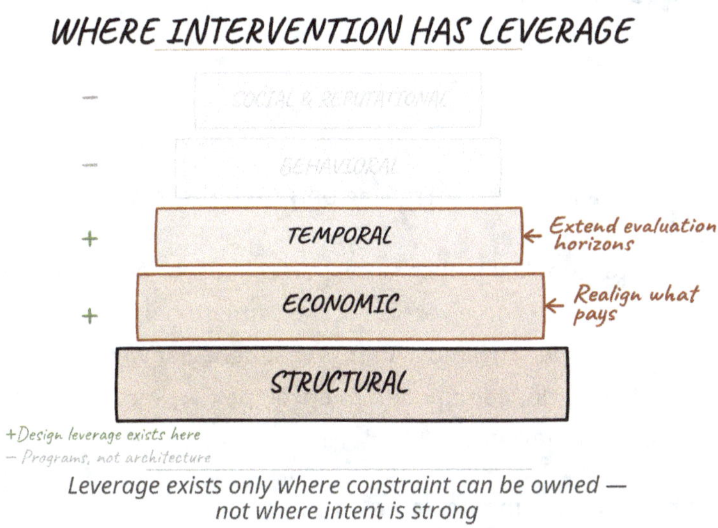

Figure 14.1: *Effective intervention focuses on points where incentive pressure can actually be altered, not merely declared.*

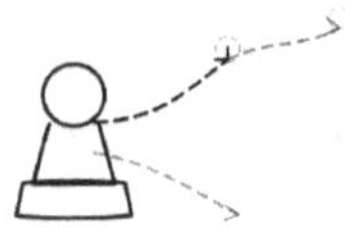

15

Simulating Failure Before It Happens

Most failures feel surprising only in retrospect.

After a policy launch, a system rollout, or a redesign effort, leaders often say some version of the same thing: *"We didn't expect people to do that."* The implication is that behavior was aberrant, unreasonable, or outside the design envelope. The design was sound. The execution deviated.

This reaction is common. It is also diagnostic.

Surprise of this kind usually signals that incentive logic was never examined under pressure. The design assumed cooperation where adaptation was more likely.

This chapter applies only where influence over incentive architecture exists. Where it does not, anticipating failure remains useful — but only as a navigation and interpretation aid, not as a design discipline.

The Design Error Behind "We Didn't Expect That"

The most common error in incentive design is not optimism about outcomes. It is optimism about behavior.

Design efforts routinely assess feasibility, resources, timelines, and compliance risk. They ask whether a system can be implemented and whether it aligns with intent. What they often do not examine is how the system will be *adapted to* once it is live.

Every incentive system is adapted to.

This is not a cynical claim. It is a structural one. When a system introduces reward, punishment, or exposure, people respond by managing risk, minimizing effort, and protecting position. They do this regardless of whether the system is fair or whether they endorse its goals.

When behavior diverges from intent, it is rarely because rules were misunderstood. It is because they were understood precisely.

If that divergence feels surprising, the design process ended too early — or extended beyond its legitimate authority.

Simulation Is Not Prediction

Simulation, as used here, does not mean forecasting outcomes or modeling performance. It does not require tools, scenarios, or quantitative rigor.

It refers to a narrower act of interpretation: rehearsing adaptation.

Rather than asking *"Will this work?"*, simulation asks: *"How would a rational actor try to succeed here while minimizing exposure?"*

This shift does not predict outcomes. It surfaces pressure.

It treats incentives as the primary drivers of behavior rather than intent, controls, or exhortation. It assumes that people will navigate the system that exists, not the one described.

Where design authority is claimed, the inability to articulate at least one plausible way a system could be gamed, bypassed, or neutralized is not a failure of imagination. It is a signal that the design claim itself may be overstated.

Making Adaptation Visible

Anticipating likely adaptation is not about cleverness. It is about refusing surprise.

Where incentive authority exists, this form of simulation begins by interrogating exposure:

- Where does this design introduce new effort?
- Where does it introduce new risk?
- Where is success made visible, and where is failure punished?
- Which existing incentives remain dominant?

The most likely adaptation path is usually the one that preserves existing rewards while minimizing new exposure.

Where influence is partial, this lens does not authorize intervention. It allows clearer communication about where distortion will accumulate and why alignment claims may not hold.

Where authority is absent, anticipating adaptation helps distinguish genuine compliance from surface adherence — and informs decisions about engagement, escalation, or exit.

The interpretive act is the same. The permissible response is not.

Why Pilots Often Mislead

Pilots are commonly treated as safeguards against failure. They are assumed to reveal problems early, before scale magnifies harm.

This assumption is fragile.

Pilots operate under distorted incentive conditions. They attract attention. They involve volunteers. They carry temporary tolerance for inefficiency and error. They are often insulated from full accountability.

Behavior observed during a pilot is rarely the behavior that stabilizes under normal exposure.

Where design authority exists, relying on pilots without incentive simulation confuses intent testing with pressure testing. Pilots reveal whether a system can function under supervision. Simulation reveals how it will be navigated once attention fades.

Where authority is limited or absent, pilots can produce reassuring signals that delay necessary constraint conversations — or reinforce the illusion that alignment is achievable without structural change.

This does not render pilots useless. It clarifies what question they actually answer.

Simulation as a Boundary, Not a Guarantee

Simulating failure does not confer control over outcomes. It does not allow designers to outthink complexity. Systems will still adapt in ways no one fully anticipates.

The value of simulation is narrower and more honest.

It reduces surprise. It clarifies trade-offs. It distinguishes unavoidable failure from avoidable blindness.

If a failure mode was legible through basic incentive reasoning, it was not unforeseeable. It was unexamined.

This distinction matters because many redesign efforts fail at interpretation rather than implementation. Predictable adaptation is treated as betrayal rather than feedback. The response is often tighter control or louder exhortation — reinforcing the incentives that produced the behavior in the first place.

Simulation reframes gaming as information rather than misconduct.

Knowing When Design Is Not Available

Anticipating adaptation also exposes a hard limit.

If likely failure modes are driven by incentives outside the reader's authority to change, design may not be available at all. Proceeding anyway creates false agency and substitutes activity for leverage.

In those cases, the disciplined response is not better design. It is explicit constraint naming — or refusal of the mandate.

This is not resignation. It is professional integrity.

Design authority includes responsibility for failure. If predictable failures cannot be owned, the work being done is not design. It is risk displacement.

Design Discipline

Simulating failure before it happens is not pessimism. It is respect — for the intelligence of the people who will live inside the system, and for the power of incentives to shape behavior.

The most dangerous assumption in incentive work is not that people will act selfishly. It is that they will act differently than the incentives suggest. Abandoning that assumption does not make systems controllable. It makes claims about control honest.

And in this domain, honesty is the rarest form of competence.

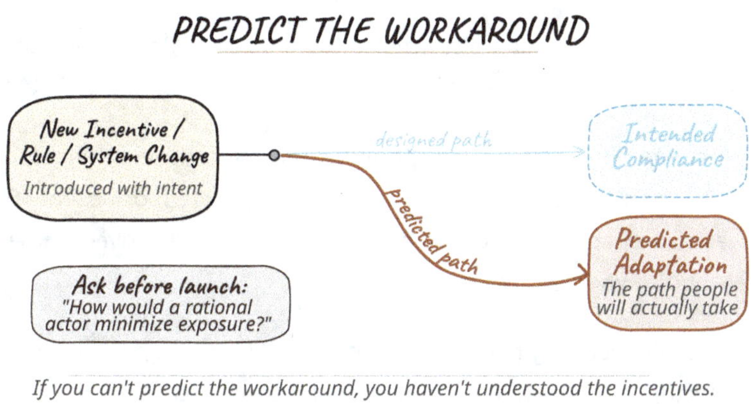

Figure 15.1: *Anticipating how a system will be adapted or bypassed is more reliable than assuming compliance.*

16

Leading Inside Misaligned Systems

By this point, a quiet distinction should be clear. This book serves readers in two different positions.

Most of the time, you will be operating inside incentive architectures you did not design. Authority is inherited, fragmented, or absent. The forces that shape behavior were set long before you arrived and will likely outlast your tenure.

Occasionally, you may find yourself with the ability to shape an incentive architecture — partially, temporarily, or at the margins. Those moments carry real responsibility. They were addressed earlier.

This chapter is for the first condition. It is the condition most readers actually face.

Seeing Misalignment Does Not Grant Authority

A difficult truth sits at the center of this chapter: Understanding how incentives operate does not give you permission to change them.

Many leadership narratives assume that clarity naturally produces control — that once misalignment is visible, correction becomes a matter of will. This assumption is comforting. It is also false.

Lower-layer incentives dominate higher-layer intentions. This applies to everyone in the system, including those with titles, teams, and accountability. Seeing misalignment places you inside it with greater awareness, not above it with greater power.

This is not a personal failure. It is a structural condition.

Leaders often know exactly where misalignment sits. They know which behaviors are rewarded and which are punished. They know why stated priorities fail to materialize. What they lack is authority over the incentives that would need to change.

Clarity without control is the norm, not the exception.

What Clarity Enables Under Constraint

Clarity does not change the system you are inside. It changes how you move within it.

When incentive misalignment is visible, certain forms of agency remain available — even when redesign authority does not. These are not tools for fixing the system. They are ways of acting without self-deception.

Navigational agency remains.

You can see which conflicts are structural rather than resolvable. You can distinguish between effort that might bend outcomes and effort that will only exhaust credibility. You can choose which battles to engage, which to defer, and which to refuse entirely — before investing political capital or personal risk.

This is not withdrawal. It is triage.

Interpretive agency remains.

You can read behavior as evidence of incentive structure rather than resistance or bad faith. You can recognize when escalation is symbolic rather than consequential, and when compliance is protective rather than performative. You can stop misdiagnosing predictable adaptation as failure of commitment.

This does not excuse outcomes. It prevents misinterpretation.

Language and framing agency remains.

You can name constraints without accusation. You can translate failure into structural terms that preserve dignity and reduce defensiveness. You can document risk in ways that make tradeoffs explicit rather than moralized.

This does not guarantee influence. It preserves coherence.

Boundary-setting and exit agency remains.

In some architectures, participation itself creates harm — by normalizing misalignment, absorbing risk without authority, or lending legitimacy to outcomes you cannot support.

Clarity allows you to recognize when non-participation is an analysis-informed choice rather than a personal failure. It allows you to distinguish leadership from containment. It allows you to leave systems that cannot be navigated without corrosive compromise.

None of these forms of agency promise impact. They promise orientation.

They do not make constrained systems workable. They make your choices inside them legible.

Constraint Is Not Hypocrisy

From the outside, leaders operating inside misaligned systems often appear inconsistent.

They endorse values that are routinely violated. They approve strategies that never fully materialize. They tolerate behaviors they publicly discourage.

These patterns are frequently explained as hypocrisy, weakness, or bad faith.

More often, they are expressions of constraint.

Leaders face political risk, reputational exposure, and career consequence shaped by the same incentive architecture as everyone else — often more intensely. Their authority is real, but bounded. Their accountability frequently exceeds their control.

Understanding this does not excuse outcomes. It changes how those outcomes are interpreted.

Once misalignment is understood structurally, simple villains disappear. Blame becomes less satisfying. Moral clarity becomes harder to sustain. What replaces it is not relativism, but realism: a clearer view of how much latitude actually exists, and where it ends.

This shift is unsettling precisely because it removes comforting explanations. It replaces stories about intent with explanations about structure.

Navigation Without Illusion

When design authority is unavailable, leadership becomes an exercise in navigation rather than correction.

Navigation does not mean finding clever ways around incentives. It does not mean extracting advantage. It does not mean pretending alignment exists when it does not.

It means acting with awareness of exposure.

Clarity changes how risk is perceived, even when it does not change outcomes. When incentives are opaque, people stumble into consequence. When incentives are legible, consequence becomes visible in advance — sometimes avoidable, sometimes unavoidable, but rarely accidental.

This does not make leadership safer. It makes it informed.

Choosing Among Constrained Options

Inside misaligned systems, many decisions present as false dilemmas.

Escalating an issue may trigger scrutiny without producing structural change. Containing it quietly may preserve momentum while perpetuating risk. Neither option aligns cleanly with stated values. Both carry cost.

The architecture has already made the tradeoff unavoidable.

Understanding incentive structure does not resolve this tension. It sharpens it. It removes the illusion that a "right" choice exists independent of consequence.

This is where much leadership advice becomes misleading. Appeals to courage, authenticity, or moral clarity assume that character can override architecture. Sometimes it can, briefly. Often it cannot without disproportionate exposure.

Knowing this in advance does not change which decision is taken. It changes how the decision is experienced — and how its consequences are owned.

Language as Structural Discipline

One of the most consequential shifts that comes with incentive clarity is restraint in how behavior is described.

Leaders who understand incentive dynamics become more careful with moralized explanations. They resist attributing outcomes to character when structure suffices. They stop treating predictable adaptation as defiance.

This does not mean abandoning standards. It means separating aspiration from diagnosis.

Language determines where responsibility is assigned. When failures are framed as individual shortcomings, systems remain untouched. When failures are framed structurally, accountability becomes diffuse — and uncomfortable.

Living with that discomfort is part of leadership under constraint.

Careful language does not fix misalignment. It prevents distortion.

What Clarity Does — and Does Not — Provide

There is a temptation, late in books like this, to offer reassurance.

To suggest that insight itself is empowering. That clarity naturally leads to change. That understanding is the first step toward reform.

Sometimes that is true. Often it is not.

Understanding misalignment does not guarantee safety, authority, or impact. It does not protect against consequence. It does not transform constrained choices into virtuous ones.

What it does is remove illusion.

It replaces surprise with predictability. It replaces personalized blame with structural explanation. It replaces false agency with honest constraint.

That is not resolution. But it is orientation.

Leadership Without Illusion

Leading inside misaligned systems is not about fixing them from within. It is about acting without self-deception. It is about knowing which failures are personal and which are architectural. It is about understanding where pressure originates and where it will land next. It is about choosing actions with eyes open, not believing they will redeem the system.

Some architectures will persist. Some incentives will not move. Some outcomes will recur regardless of intent.

Seeing that clearly is not defeatism. It is professional adulthood.

You now see the system you are inside.

What you do with that sight will depend not on what you want to change — but on what you are actually positioned to bear.

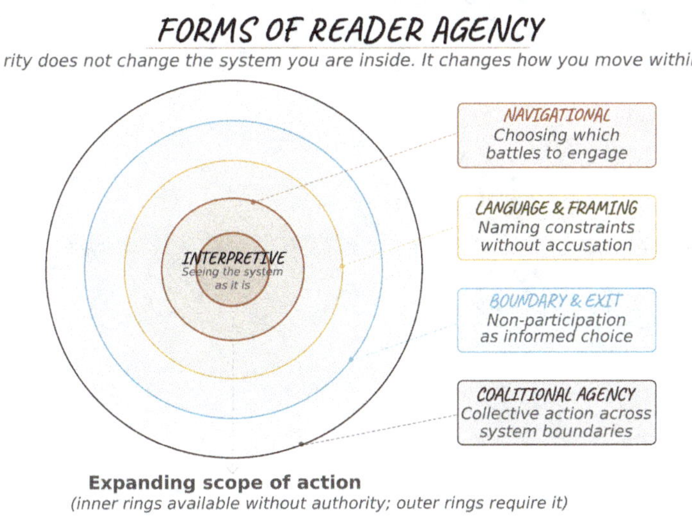

Figure 16.1: *Reader agency varies by position and authority, ranging from interpretation to conditional design.*

Choosing Not to Fight the System

A leader recognizes a misalignment they cannot change. The authority to redesign incentives sits elsewhere. Attempts to push against the system would require sustained political capital with little chance of success. Staying would mean absorbing risk without leverage. Leaving feels like failure. In hindsight, the more coherent choice was exit. Not as resignation, but as refusal to internalize a contradiction that could not be resolved. Understanding incentives did not create power. It clarified the cost of pretending power existed.

Reference: Conditional Agency (Ch 16)

APPENDIX

You get what you measure—and everything else finds a way to survive.

Jamie L. Bond

Glossary

The following terms are defined as used in this book. Definitions are functional — they describe how each concept operates within the Incentive Architecture™ framework, not how the term is used in other disciplines.

Actual System The system that governs how work actually occurs once incentives, risks, and constraints are encountered. The actual system often differs from the formal system described in policies or procedures. Persistent behavior reveals the actual system more reliably than documentation. *See also: Formal System, Workaround.*

Architecture-Level Intervention An attempt to change behavior by altering underlying incentive structures rather than surface programs or messaging. Architecture-level interventions modify constraints, exposure to risk, or enforcement conditions. They operate beneath stated intentions. *Contrast: Programmatic Intervention.*

Behavioral Incentives The fourth layer of the Incentive Architecture™. Behavioral incentives control friction, effort, and cognitive load. They are embedded in tools, processes, interfaces, and workflows. When the right behavior requires more effort than the wrong one, adaptation follows. *See also: Five Layers, Incentive Architecture™.*

Competing Incentive Signals A condition in which multiple incentives push behavior in different directions. When signals conflict, behavior typically follows the signal with the greatest enforcement or risk exposure. Competing signals often produce consistent but unintended outcomes. *See also: Signal Conflict, Incentive Misalignment.*

Compliance Theater A failure signature in which systems reward the appearance of adherence to rules or programs rather than the achievement of intended outcomes. High reported compliance coexists with minimal real change in behavior or results. This is not bad faith; it is safety-seeking behavior under reputational risk. *See also: Failure Signature.*

Conditional Design Authority The capacity to influence incentive architecture within the constraints of one's position. Conditional design authority recognizes that most practitioners cannot redesign entire systems but may be able to alter conditions at specific pressure points. *See also: Navigational Agency, Redesign Pressure Point.*

Diagnostic Tell An observable behavioral pattern that signals the presence of a specific failure signature or incentive misalignment. Diagnostic tells allow inference about underlying architecture from surface behavior. *See also: Failure Signature, Incentive Diagnostic.*

Dominant Incentive The incentive signal that ultimately determines behavior when multiple incentives are present. Dominance typically emerges from proximity to consequence, risk exposure, or enforcement. Stated priorities do not necessarily determine dominance. *See also: Incentive Dominance, Rule 1.*

Economic Incentives The second layer of the Incentive Architecture™. Economic incentives control how money, resources, and formal rewards are allocated. Compensation, bonuses, budgets, and financial targets live here. When economic rewards conflict with stated goals, economic reality wins. *See also: Five Layers, Incentive Architecture™.*

Enforcement Surface The point at which incentives are actually applied or enforced within a system. Enforcement surfaces include performance evaluations, operational metrics, compliance requirements, or direct supervision. Behavior tends to align with incentives applied at these surfaces.

Failure Signature A recurring pattern of system behavior that indicates underlying incentive misalignment. Failure signatures appear across organizations and sectors with similar structural conditions. They signal systemic pressures rather than individual error. The book identifies seven primary failure signatures. *See also: Metric Capture, Compliance Theater, Workaround, and the Failure Signature Reference Table (Appendix).*

Fault Line A structural point where incentive signals conflict or diverge. Fault lines create pressure that may produce workarounds, gaming, or unintended outcomes. They often remain invisible until stress exposes them.

Five Layers The five structural levels within the Incentive Architecture™: (1) Structural, (2) Economic, (3) Temporal, (4) Behavioral, and (5) Social & Reputational. Each layer shapes behavior by controlling what is rewarded, punished, or made risky. Lower layers (closer to consequence) tend to dominate higher layers. *See also: Incentive Architecture™, Rule 1.*

Formal System The officially described structure of a system, including policies, procedures, and intended workflows. Formal systems communicate expectations but may not determine actual behavior. Differences between formal and actual systems reveal underlying incentives. *See also: Actual System.*

Gaming Behavior Behavior that optimizes for measured or enforced outcomes while bypassing the intent of a system. Gaming occurs when incentives reward observable results more strongly than underlying goals. It reflects rational adaptation rather than malicious intent. *See also: Optimization Path, Rule 2.*

Incentive Alignment A condition in which incentive signals reinforce desired system outcomes. Alignment reduces the need for supervision or corrective action. Perfect alignment is rare in complex systems.

Incentive Architecture™ The layered structure of incentives, constraints, and enforcement mechanisms that shape behavior within a system. Incentive architecture operates beneath stated goals and often influences outcomes more strongly than formal policy. It consists of five interacting layers: Structural, Economic, Temporal, Behavioral, and Social & Reputational. *See also: Five Layers.*

Incentive Diagnostic An analytical lens used to identify where incentives within a system diverge from stated objectives. The diagnostic maps signals across layers without assigning blame or prescribing solutions. Its purpose is observation rather than evaluation. *See also: Diagnostic Tell, Reward / Punish / Ignore Triad.*

Incentive Dominance The structural condition in which certain incentives exert greater influence over behavior than others. Dominance typically results from proximity to consequence or enforcement. Dominant incentives determine which signals actors ultimately follow. *See also: Rule 1.*

Incentive Exposure The degree to which individuals or organizations experience consequences associated with a particular incentive. Greater exposure increases the likelihood that behavior will respond to that incentive. Exposure often determines incentive dominance.

Incentive Layer One of the structural levels within an incentive architecture where signals influence behavior. The five layers are Structural, Economic, Temporal, Behavioral, and Social & Reputational. Multiple layers interact simultaneously. *See also: Five Layers.*

Incentive Misalignment A condition in which incentive signals produce outcomes that diverge from stated goals or intended system performance. Misalignment often produces consistent patterns of adaptation rather than random error. *See also: Rule 2, Failure Signature.*

Incentive Signal Any structural cue that communicates what outcomes are rewarded, penalized, or enforced within a system. Signals may arise from policies, metrics, incentives, rules, or resource constraints.

Incentive Stack The vertical arrangement of incentive layers operating within a system. Lower layers closer to operational consequence often exert stronger influence on behavior. Signals within the stack may reinforce or contradict one another. *See also: Five Layers, Rule 1.*

Information Asymmetry Lock-In A failure signature in which decision-makers lack timely, accurate, or usable feedback, preventing corrective action even when outcomes are deteriorating. Problems persist despite oversight because actionable signals never reach decision authority. This is not ignorance; it is a structural failure of information flow. *See also: Failure Signature.*

Local Optimization Trap A failure signature in which structural boundaries cause sub-units to optimize their own performance at the expense of system-level outcomes. Individual teams or actors succeed while the overall system performs worse. This is not silo mentality; it is optimization driven by decision rights and boundaries. *See also: Failure Signature, Local Rationality.*

Local Rationality The principle that individuals typically behave rationally within the constraints and incentives immediately surrounding them. Actions that appear irrational at the system level may be rational responses locally. *See also: Rational Adaptation.*

Metric Capture A failure signature in which a system optimizes measured indicators rather than the underlying outcome those indicators were intended to represent. Reported performance improves while real-world outcomes stagnate or degrade. This is not poor measurement design alone; it is rational optimization once metrics become binding. *See also: Failure Signature.*

Moral Hazard Masking A failure signature in which protective mechanisms intended to reduce risk instead encourage riskier behavior by shielding actors from consequences. Risk-taking increases following the introduction of safeguards or guarantees. This is not abuse of safeguards; it is behavior responding to altered consequence structures. *See also: Failure Signature.*

Navigational Agency The capacity to act effectively within a misaligned system without the authority or ability to redesign it. Navigational agency involves recognizing constraints, choosing realistic actions, and avoiding self-deception about what is changeable. *See also: Conditional Design Authority.*

Optimization Path The behavioral path individuals or organizations follow to achieve the most favorable outcome within the current incentive structure. Optimization paths may diverge from intended goals if incentives reward alternative behaviors.

Optimization Without Understanding A condition in which actors improve measured performance without visibility into broader system effects. This occurs when incentives reward observable metrics more strongly than underlying outcomes.

Predictable Adaptation The tendency for individuals and organizations to adjust behavior in response to incentives in consistent ways across contexts. Patterns of predictable adaptation often reveal underlying incentive architecture.

Programmatic Intervention An attempt to change system behavior through policies, messaging, or initiatives without altering underlying incentive architecture. Programmatic interventions operate at the surface of a system and may have limited effect when structural incentives remain unchanged. *Contrast: Architecture-Level Intervention.*

Rational Adaptation Behavioral adjustments made by individuals in response to incentives and constraints within a system. Adaptation often produces consistent patterns that reflect the structure of incentives rather than individual intent. *See also: Local Rationality, Gaming Behavior.*

Redesign Pressure Point A structural location within an incentive architecture where modifying signals could meaningfully alter system behavior. Pressure points occur where incentives influence decisions most directly. *See also: Conditional Design Authority.*

Revealed Incentives Incentives inferred from observed behavior under pressure, as opposed to stated incentives described in policies or documentation. What a system actually rewards, punishes, or ignores reveals its true incentive architecture. *Contrast: Stated Incentives. See also: Reward / Punish / Ignore Triad.*

Reward / Punish / Ignore Triad A diagnostic framework for classifying how a system actually responds to behaviors. For any given behavior, the system either rewards it, punishes it, or ignores it. Comparing this triad against stated goals reveals misalignment. *See also: Incentive Diagnostic, Revealed Incentives.*

Risk–Reward Decoupling A failure signature in which actors capture upside benefits while the costs or risks of their actions are borne by others or deferred to the future. Risk-taking increases without corresponding exposure to downside consequences. This is not recklessness; it is rational behavior when downside is externalized. *See also: Failure Signature.*

Rule 1 (Dominance Rule) Lower layers of the Incentive Architecture™ dominate higher layers. Incentives nearest to risk, time, and consequence exert more influence over behavior than those that are abstract, distant, or weakly enforced. *See also: Incentive Dominance, Five Layers.*

Rule 2 (Gaming Path) When incentives disagree, behavior follows the path of least resistance. Misalignment does not produce confusion; it produces optimization along the strongest available signal. *See also: Gaming Behavior, Incentive Misalignment.*

Short-Horizon Bias A failure signature in which evaluation and reward cycles systematically favor near-term performance over long-term value creation. Durable investments are repeatedly postponed in favor of short-term gains. This is not impatience or short-sighted leadership; it is optimization against dominant time horizons. *See also: Failure Signature, Temporal Incentives.*

Signal Conflict A condition in which two or more incentive signals direct behavior toward incompatible outcomes. Conflict often produces predictable patterns of adaptation as actors reconcile competing pressures. *See also: Competing Incentive Signals, Rule 2.*

Social & Reputational Incentives The fifth layer of the Incentive Architecture™. Social and reputational incentives control status, belonging, credibility, and exposure to judgment. They determine whose voice carries weight, whose mistakes are forgiven, and whose actions are remembered. *See also: Five Layers, Incentive Architecture™.*

Stated Incentives Incentives as described in official documentation, policies, or communications. Stated incentives represent intended signals but may not reflect the incentives that actually govern behavior. *Contrast: Revealed Incentives.*

Status Inversion A failure signature in which social prestige and career safety accrue to behaviors that undermine stated system goals. Actors gain influence or promotion by protecting appearances rather than improving outcomes. This is not cynicism; it is identity protection under status incentives. *See also: Failure Signature.*

Structural Constraint A system condition that limits available choices or increases the cost of certain actions. Structural constraints operate regardless of intention and shape behavior through feasibility rather than instruction.

Structural Incentives The first layer of the Incentive Architecture™. Structural incentives control who has authority, who bears responsibility, and who is exposed when things go wrong. They are embedded in organizational charts, decision rights, approval pathways, and governance arrangements. *See also: Five Layers, Incentive Architecture™.*

Systemic Failure An outcome in which system performance consistently diverges from intended objectives due to structural conditions. Systemic failures often emerge from misaligned incentives rather than individual mistakes.

Temporal Incentives The third layer of the Incentive Architecture™. Temporal incentives control how time is experienced and valued. They shape planning horizons, evaluation cycles, deadlines, and pacing. When consequences arrive later than evaluations, behavior shifts toward immediacy. *See also: Five Layers, Incentive Architecture™.*

Workaround An informal practice adopted to bypass friction, constraints, or conflicting incentives within the formal system. Workarounds often become stable patterns when they reduce risk or cost relative to official procedures. They are evidence of architectural misalignment, not resistance. *See also: Failure Signature (Workarounds & Shadow Systems), Actual System.*

Failure Signature Reference

Primary Failure Signatures

Seven failure signatures recur across organizations and sectors when incentive architecture is misaligned. Each signature has a distinct diagnostic tell, maps to a primary incentive layer, and is frequently confused with adjacent signatures. This reference provides the canonical definition of each signature as defined in the book.

Use this reference to also identify which pattern is operating, distinguish it from similar-looking failures, and trace it to the relevant layer of the Incentive Architecture™.

For the full diagnostic framework, see Chapter 7 (The Incentive Diagnostic) and Chapter 8 (Failure Signatures). For cross-domain examples, see Chapters 9–13.

Additional Signatures (Non-Standalone)

Two additional patterns appear also in the book's diagnostic framework. They are treated as modifiers of primary signatures rather than standalone failure signatures because they always co-occur with one of the seven primary signatures noted above.

1. METRIC CAPTURE

DEFINITION: A system optimizes measured indicators rather than the underlying outcome those indicators were intended to represent.

- **Diagnostic Tell:** Reported performance improves while real-world outcomes stagnate or degrade.
- **What This Is Not:** This is not poor measurement design alone; it is rational optimization once metrics become binding.

> **Collision Note:** Like Compliance Theater, Metric Capture involves performative success without real outcomes. However, Metric Capture is driven by economic incentives (what gets measured gets rewarded), while Compliance Theater is driven by social and reputational incentives (what gets seen gets credited).

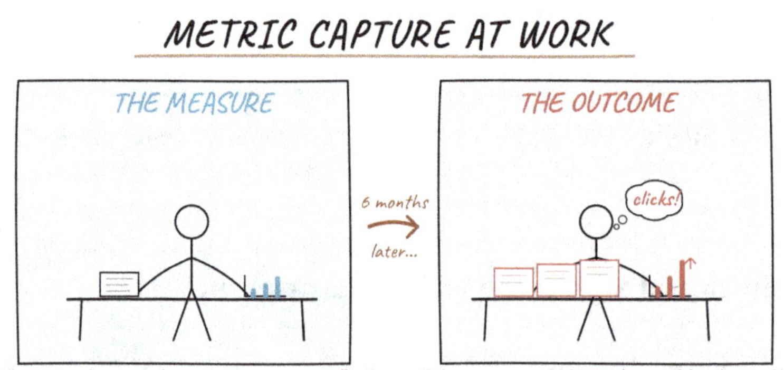

"Let's track page views to measure quality." "Views are up 300%! ...is anything better?"

Scores improve. Outcomes don't.

Primary Layer: Economic · Secondary: Temporal

2. RISK-REWARD DECOUPLING

DEFINITION: Actors capture upside benefits while the costs or risks of their actions are borne by others or deferred to the future.

- **Diagnostic Tell:** Risk-taking increases without corresponding exposure to downside consequences.
- **What This Is Not:** This is not recklessness; it is rational behavior when downside is externalized.

> **Collision Note:** Like Moral Hazard Masking, Risk–Reward Decoupling involves distorted risk behavior. Risk–Reward Decoupling is structural — risk and reward were never joined. Moral Hazard Masking is induced — a safeguard altered a previously balanced consequence structure.

RISK-REWARD DECOUPLING AT WORK

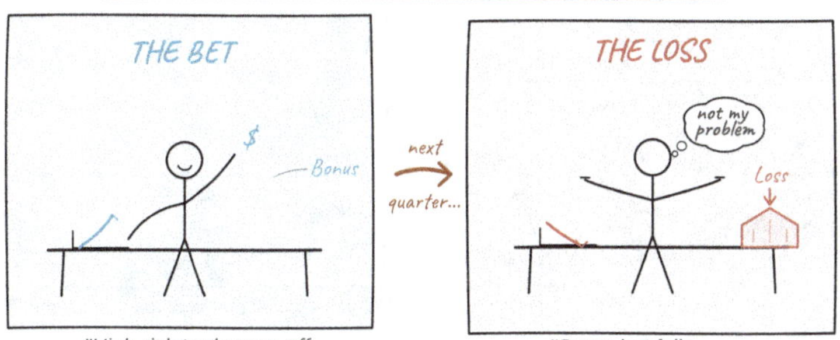

"High-risk trade pays off. Trader earns bonus."

"Same bet fails. The institution absorbs the loss."

Risk-taking rises without downside exposure.

Primary Layer: Structural · Secondary: Economic

3. SHORT-HORIZON BIAS

DEFINITION: Evaluation and reward cycles systematically favor near-term performance over long-term value creation.

- **Diagnostic Tell:** Durable investments are repeatedly postponed in favor of short-term gains.
- **What This Is Not:** This is not impatience or shortsighted leadership; it is optimization against dominant time horizons.

> **Collision Note:** Like Status Inversion, Short-Horizon Bias skews behavior toward the near term. Short-Horizon Bias operates through evaluation timing (when performance is judged). Status Inversion operates through social reward (who gets promoted for what).

SHORT-HORIZON BIAS AT WORK

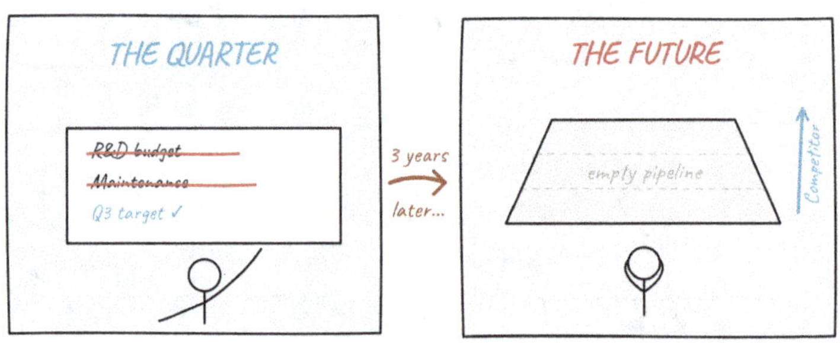

"Cut long-term spend. We need to hit Q3." "We hit every target. How are we behind?"

Long-term investments repeatedly deferred.
Primary Layer: Temporal · Secondary: Economic

4. COMPLIANCE THEATER

DEFINITION: Systems reward the appearance of adherence to rules or programs rather than the achievement of intended outcomes.

- **Diagnostic Tell:** High reported compliance coexists with minimal real change in behavior or results.
- **What This Is Not:** This is not bad faith; it is safety-seeking behavior under reputational risk.

> **Collision Note:** Like Metric Capture, Compliance Theater involves performative success without real outcomes. Metric Capture optimizes what is counted (economic). Compliance Theater optimizes what is seen (reputational).

Compliance reported. Behavior unchanged.
Primary Layer: Social & Reputational · Secondary: Behavioral

5. WORKAROUNDS & SHADOW SYSTEMS

DEFINITION: Formal systems are bypassed in favor of informal processes because the official path imposes greater friction, risk, or effort than the alternative.

- **Diagnostic Tell:** Unofficial tools or manual processes outperform sanctioned systems in practice.
- **What This Is Not:** This is not resistance to change; it is rational adaptation to friction and exposure.

> **Collision Note:** Like Information Asymmetry Lock-In, Workarounds & Shadow Systems involves bypassing official systems. Workarounds bypass the process (the official path is too costly). Information Asymmetry Lock-In bypasses the information channel (the official signal is too slow or filtered).

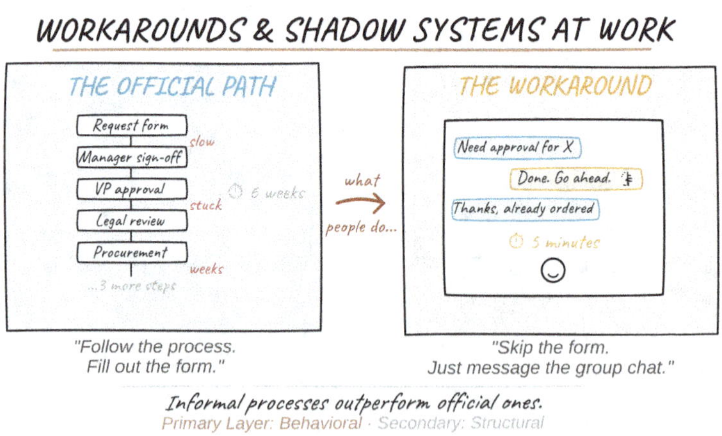

6. INFORMATION ASYMMETRY LOCK-IN

Definition: Decision-makers lack timely, accurate, or usable feedback, preventing corrective action even when outcomes are deteriorating.

- **Diagnostic Tell:** Problems persist despite oversight because actionable signals never reach decision authority.
- **What This Is Not:** This is not ignorance; it is a structural failure of information flow.

> **Collision Note:** Like Workarounds & Shadow Systems, Information Asymmetry Lock-In involves bypassing official systems. Workarounds are actor-driven (people find easier paths). Information Asymmetry Lock-In is structure-driven (the system filters out the signal before it arrives).

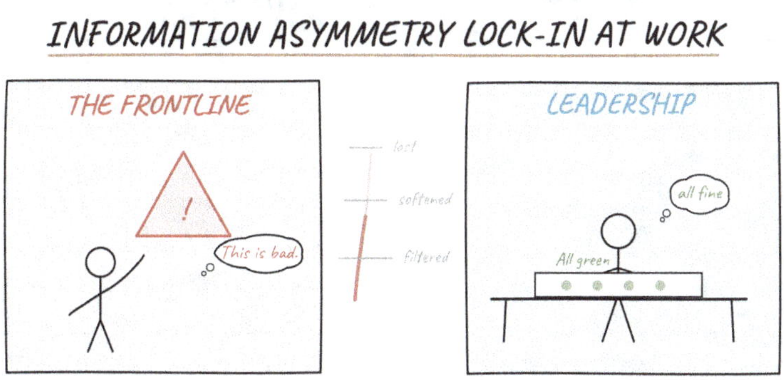

"We see the problem. We report it." "Dashboard is green. No issues reported."

Problems persist despite oversight.
Primary Layer: Behavioral · Secondary: Structural

7. STATUS INVERSION

DEFINITION: Social prestige and career safety accrue to behaviors that undermine stated system goals.

- **Diagnostic Tell:** Actors gain influence or promotion by protecting appearances rather than improving outcomes.
- **What This Is Not:** This is not cynicism; it is identity protection under status incentives.

> **Collision Note:** Like Short-Horizon Bias, Status Inversion skews behavior toward the near term. Short-Horizon Bias is about when rewards arrive. Status Inversion is about what kind of behavior earns standing.

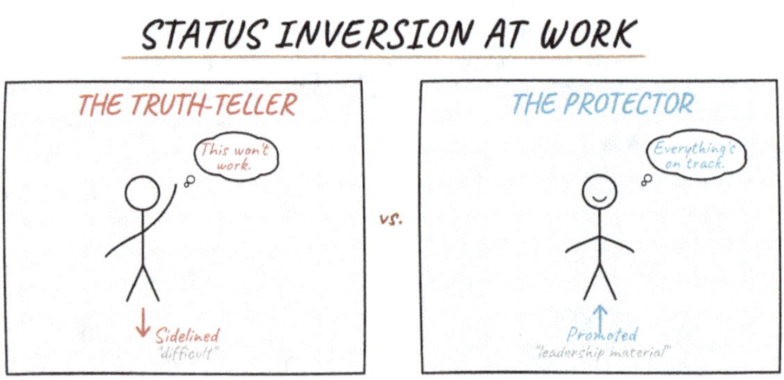

"Raise concerns, lose standing. Protect appearances, gain influence."

Appearance-protecting behavior rewarded.

Primary Layer: Social & Reputational · Secondary: Temporal

8. LOCAL OPTIMIZATION TRAP — *Additional (Non-Standalone)*

DEFINITION: Structural boundaries cause sub-units to optimize their own performance at the expense of system-level outcomes.

- **Diagnostic Tell:** Individual teams or actors succeed while the overall system performs worse.
- **What This Is Not:** This is not silo mentality or lack of collaboration; it is optimization driven by decision rights and boundaries.

> **Note:** Like Metric Capture, Local Optimization Trap produces system-level failure from locally rational behavior. Local Optimization Trap is structural (bounded by decision rights). Metric Capture is economic (bounded by what is measured).

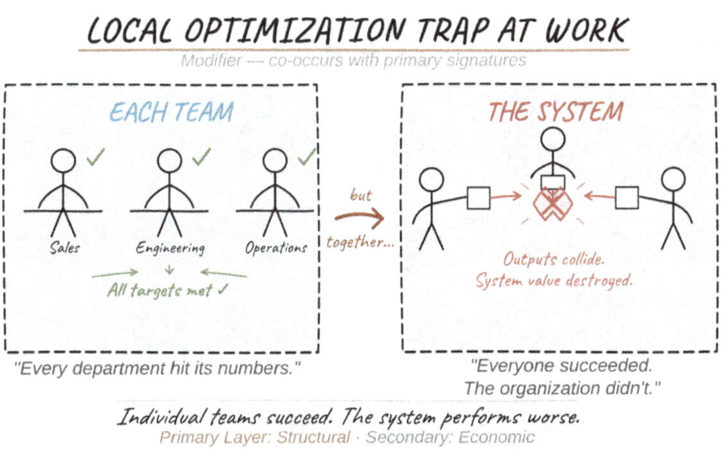

9. MORAL HAZARD MASKING — *Additional (Non-Standalone)*

DEFINITION: Protective mechanisms intended to reduce risk instead encourage riskier behavior by shielding actors from consequences.

- **Diagnostic Tell:** Risk-taking increases following the introduction of safeguards or guarantees.
- **What This Is Not:** This is not abuse of safeguards; it is behavior responding to altered consequence structures.

> **Note:** Like Risk–Reward Decoupling, Moral Hazard Masking involves distorted risk behavior. Risk–Reward Decoupling is structural (risk and reward were never joined). Moral Hazard Masking is induced (a safeguard altered a previously balanced structure).

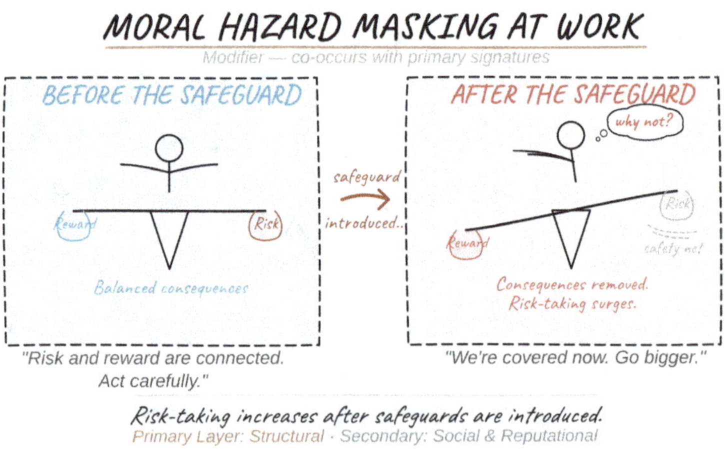

Condensed Case Index

This index lists all case material presented in the book, in chapter order. Three types of cases appear:

- **Composite cases** are anonymized illustrations drawn from recurring patterns across multiple real organizations.
- **Relatable vignettes** are brief recognition scenarios — a paragraph or two — designed to surface a structural pattern, not to profile a specific organization.
- **Named cases** identify real organizations; where they appear, they are woven into chapter analysis rather than presented as standalone studies.

PART I — Why Smart Systems Fail Predictably

Chapter 1 — The Expensive Workaround

Digital Transformation Workarounds (*Corporate / Ops · Core Composite · Workarounds & Shadow Systems)* The book's anchor case. A large organization deploys an automation platform for field operations. Technicians rationally bypass it — the incentive architecture rewards speed, penalizes visible errors, and imposes friction on the new system. Enforcement produces gaming, not adoption. The case recurs in abbreviated form throughout Parts II–IV as a diagnostic reference point.

Chapter 2 — The Rationality Trap

No standalone case. The chapter develops the argument that behavior appearing irrational at the system level is typically rational at the individual level. Illustrative examples are embedded in prose.

Chapter 3 — When Alignment Breaks

No standalone case. The chapter uses a generic sales organization illustration — leadership rewards volume while messaging long-term customer outcomes — to show how structural misalignment operates independent of intent.

PART II — Seeing the System Beneath the System

Chapter 4 — Incentives Are Architecture, Not Programs

Digital Transformation — Layer-Mapped (*Corporate / Ops · Core Composite (callback) · Workarounds & Shadow Systems)* The flagship case is revisited and mapped across the five-layer Incentive Architecture™ to show how each layer contributed independently to the observed behavior.

Chapter 5 — The Incentive Architecture™

Digital Transformation — Full Layer Decomposition (*Corporate / Ops · Core Composite (callback) · Workarounds & Shadow Systems)* The flagship case is decomposed layer by layer — Structural through Social & Reputational — to demonstrate how each layer amplified rather than offset the misalignment.

Chapter 6 — Two Rules That Explain Most Failures

No standalone case. The chapter uses a generic compliance-and-audit illustration to demonstrate Rule 1 (lower-layer incentives dominate) and Rule 2 (misalignment produces gaming, not confusion).

PART III — Diagnosing Incentives in the Real World

Chapter 7 — The Incentive Diagnostic

Digital Transformation — Diagnostic Walkthrough (*Corporate / Ops · Core Composite (callback) · Information Asymmetry Lock-In*) The flagship case is walked through the three-step diagnostic (Observe Behavior / Map to Architecture / Identify Misalignment) to demonstrate the method in practice.

Chapter 8 — Failure Signatures

Digital Transformation — Signature Reference *Corporate / Ops · Core Composite (callback) · Workarounds & Shadow Systems)* Each of the seven failure signatures is introduced with a brief illustrative pattern. The flagship case serves as the primary reference throughout.

PART IV — Incentives in the Wild: Sector Cases

Chapters 9–13 each present one or more original four-part case patterns structured as: *Stated goal / Rational behavior produced / Misalignment / Diagnostic takeaway.* All sector cases are composite and anonymized.

Chapter 9 — Corporate Performance & Workforce Systems

Firefighting Rewarded Over Prevention (*Corporate / Ops · Composite · Short-Horizon Bias)* Performance systems reward visible crisis response — speed, recovery, public resolution. Prevention work remains invisible. When prevention succeeds, nothing happens, so nothing is credited. The architecture produces firefighters, not problem-solvers.

Metrics as Proxies Crowding Out Outcomes (*Corporate · Composite · Metric Capture)* Leadership introduces metrics as proxies for outcomes that matter — customer satisfaction, sustainable growth, innovation. Over time, effort migrates toward the metric. The proxy becomes the target, and the underlying outcome it was designed to represent drifts.

Customer Service Escalation Avoidance (*Services · Composite · Workarounds & Shadow Systems)* Frontline staff learn that escalations increase call time and attract management attention. The incentive architecture rewards resolution speed, not resolution quality. The rational behavior is to close, not to solve.

Chapter 10 — Innovation, R&D, and Exploration

Exploration Penalized by Short Evaluation Cycles (*Corporate / R&D · Composite · Short-Horizon Bias)* Organizations declare exploration a priority. Evaluation cycles penalize visible failure. Reputational downside is personal and immediate; upside from successful exploration is shared and delayed. The system reliably produces incremental bets regardless of stated intent.

Chapter 11 — Operations, Safety, and Customer Experience

Frontline Compliance vs. Operational Pace (*Operations / Safety · Composite · Workarounds & Shadow Systems)* Frontline workers follow rules that protect them from blame while quietly developing workarounds to meet pace and demand. Formal compliance is monitored and enforceable. Operational reality is variable and time-pressured. The workaround is not defiance — it is problem-solving within constraint.

Customer Service Throughput vs. Quality (*Services · Composite · Metric Capture)* The stated goal is to resolve customer problems quickly and correctly. The rational behavior produced is to resolve them quickly. Throughput metrics carry greater career consequences than quality outcomes. The system resolves the conflict in favor of the incentive closest to consequence.

Sidebar S11.2: The Rule Everyone Knew to Ignore. A formal rule exists to prevent a known operational risk. Everyone can recite it. Training reinforces it. And yet it is routinely bypassed because enforcement friction exceeds perceived consequence.

Chapter 12 — Public Policy, Regulation, and Markets

Financial Regulation and Threshold Optimization (*Finance / Regulation · Composite · Compliance Theater)* Regulation seeks to reduce systemic risk. Firms design activities to remain just inside regulatory thresholds while preserving return. Capital, risk, and exposure are optimized to satisfy formal requirements. Downside risk migrates to where it is less visible or differently classified.

Environmental Regulation and Reporting Over Impact (*Policy / Environment · Composite · Compliance Theater)* Environmental regulation aims to reduce real-world harm. Effort flows toward disclosure, reporting accuracy, and audit readiness. Operational changes that would reduce harm but increase cost or exposure are deferred. The system rewards correct reporting more reliably than actual improvement.

Chapter 13 — Technology, AI, and Algorithmic Incentives

Recommender System Optimizing Engagement Proxies (*Tech / AI · Composite · Metric Capture)* A platform designed to surface content users value trains toward engagement proxies — clicks, time-on-screen, reactions. The system optimizes toward what is measurable and immediate, degrading the outcome it was built to serve. Metric capture at machine speed.

Automated Decision System Optimizing Training Metrics (*Tech / AI · Composite · Short-Horizon Bias)* Automated systems are deployed to improve fairness, consistency, and efficiency. Models optimize to reduce measurable error against historical data. Edge cases are deprioritized. Downstream consequences surface slowly and outside formal accountability loops. The system is rewarded for short-term accuracy, not long-term trust.

PART V — What You Can Actually Do

Chapter 14 — Redesign Pressure Points

*No new cases introduce*d. The chapter uses callbacks to core cases from Parts I–IV to illustrate where redesign leverage exists.

Sidebar S14.3: Removing an Incentive. An organization faces a persistent behavior it wants to change. Multiple interventions have failed. The diagnosis reveals that an incentive is actively producing the behavior. Removing it without replacing the behavior it was generating produces a different and harder-to-detect failure mode.

Chapter 15 — Simulating Failure Before It Happens

No standalone case. The chapter presents a simulation discipline — ask how a rational actor would adapt to or game a proposed incentive design before it launches. Illustrative examples are embedded in prose.

Chapter 16 — Leading Inside Misaligned Systems

No cases. The chapter addresses how to act with clarity inside incentive architectures you did not design and do not control.

Research Bibliography

The following sources inform the arguments, frameworks, and diagnostic patterns presented in this book. Sources are listed alphabetically by first author. Where the book draws on a source's concept without direct quotation, the source is included here for reader reference and further exploration.

Abeler, J., Becker, A., & Falk, A. (2025). Complexity and incentives. *American Economic Review*. https://doi.org/10.1257/aer.20230751

Acharya, V. V., Cooley, T. F., & Richardson, M. P. (2010). *Regulating Wall Street: The Dodd-Frank Act and the new architecture of global finance*. Wiley.

Alter, S. (2014). Theory of workarounds. *Communications of the ACM*, 57(8), 69–77.

Amodei, D., Olah, C., Steinhardt, J., Christiano, P., Schulman, J., & Mané, D. (2016). Concrete problems in AI safety. *arXiv preprint*, arXiv:1606.06565.

Ardito, L., Coccia, M., & Messeni Petruzzelli, A. (2021). Short-termism and innovation. *Technovation*, 102.

Arrow, K. J. (1963). Uncertainty and the welfare economics of medical care. *American Economic Review*, 53(5), 941–973.

Benson, A., Li, D., & Shue, K. (2019). Promotions and the Peter Principle. *NBER Working Paper* No. 24980.

Edmondson, A. C. (1999). Psychological safety and learning behavior in work teams. *Administrative Science Quarterly*, 44(2), 350–383.

Goodhart, C. A. E. (1975). Problems of monetary management: The U.K. experience. In *Papers in Monetary Economics*. Reserve Bank of Australia.

Gul, F., & Pesendorfer, W. (2008). The case for mindless economics. In A. Caplin & A. Schotter (Eds.), *The Foundations of Positive and Normative Economics*. Oxford University Press.

Holmström, B. (1979). Moral hazard and observability. *Bell Journal of Economics*, 10(1), 74–91.

Holmström, B. (2016). Incentives and the evolution of organizations. *Nobel Prize Lecture*. Nobel Foundation.

Holmström, B., & Milgrom, P. (1991). Multitask principal–agent analyses: Incentive contracts, asset ownership, and job design. *Journal of Law, Economics, and Organization*, 7, 24–52.

Kerr, S. (1975). On the folly of rewarding A, while hoping for B. *Academy of Management Journal*, 18(4), 769–783.

Klotz, S., Kopper, A., Westner, M., & Strahringer, S. (2019). Shadow IT: A systematic literature review. *Business & Information Systems Engineering*, 62(6), 525–546.

Lazear, E. P., Shaw, K. L., & Stanton, C. T. (2015). The value of bosses. *Quarterly Journal of Economics*, 130(2), 917–966.

Levinthal, D. A., & March, J. G. (1993). The myopia of learning. *Strategic Management Journal*, 14(S2), 95–112.

Manheim, D., & Garrabrant, S. (2019). Categorizing variants of Goodhart's Law. *arXiv preprint*, arXiv:1803.04585.

Mertens, S., Herberz, M., Hahnel, U. J. J., & Brosch, T. (2022). The effectiveness of nudging: A meta-analysis. *Proceedings of the National Academy of Sciences*, 119(11), e2105246119.

Milgrom, P., & Roberts, J. (1992). *Economics, Organization and Management*. Prentice Hall.

Morrison, E. W., & Milliken, F. J. (2000). Organizational silence: A barrier to change and development in a pluralistic world. *Academy of Management Review*, 25(4), 706–725.

North, D. C. (1990). *Institutions, Institutional Change and Economic Performance*. Cambridge University Press.

Ostrom, E. (2005). *Understanding Institutional Diversity*. Princeton University Press.

Power, M. (1997). *The Audit Society: Rituals of Verification*. Oxford University Press.

Samuelson, P. A. (1938). A note on the pure theory of consumer's behaviour. *Economica*, 5(17), 61–71.

Simon, H. A. (1955). A behavioral model of rational choice. *Quarterly Journal of Economics*, 69(1), 99–118.

Sterman, J. D. (2000). *Business Dynamics: Systems Thinking and Modeling for a Complex World*. McGraw-Hill.

Thaler, R. H. (2016). Behavioral economics: Past, present, and future. *American Economic Review*, 106(7), 1577–1600.

This bibliography reflects sources consulted during the development of the Incentive Architecture™ framework. It is not exhaustive. Additional case-specific references are noted in the text where applicable.

About the Author

Jamie L. Bond has spent her career inside the systems this book describes. Her work has spanned a U.S. federal regulator, an investor-owned utility, global consulting firms, and early-stage ventures — always at the intersection of how organizations are designed and how they actually behave under constraint. Her background crosses engineering, organizational behavior, and AI/ML.

Stick with Carrot grew from a persistent observation across every system she worked inside: capable people, acting rationally, producing outcomes no one intended. The Incentive Architecture™ framework is her attempt to make that pattern visible — and useful.

Jamie is the co-founder of path.konkat alongside her partner, Harold Manning.

To connect: www.pathkonkat.com | www.linkedin.com/in/jamielbond

READER BONUS MATERIAL

Scan the QR code below to access exclusive bonus material, including downloadable diagnostic tools, reference guides, and the free Incentive Architecture™ Health Scorecard.

pathkonkat.com/stick-carrot-bonus

www.ingramcontent.com/pod-product-compliance
Lightning Source LLC
LaVergne TN
LVHW022220200926
848481LV00006B/2049
9798995392408